I'm "Fred"
The Fred Peschl Story

by
Fred Peschl and Gary A. Goreham

Published by Harold's Printing Co., Brookings, SD

I'm "Fred": The Fred Peschl Story
by Fred Peschl and Gary A. Goreham
Copyright © 1999 by Fred Peschl

ISBN: 0-9673814-0-1

Published by
Harold's Printing Co.
216 Fifth Avenue
Brookings, SD 57006

Table of Contents

List of Illustrations ii

List of Maps iii

Acknowledgments iv

Introduction v

1. Paratrooper Training 1

2. Preparing for D-Day 16

3. D-Day 24

4. Captured! 31

5. Stalag Luft IV 38

6. The Long March 50

7. Liberated 54

8. Home Again 62

9. Life Goes On 65

Epilogue 70

Chronology 71

References 73

List of Illustrations

507th Parachute Infantry training
   at Ft. Benning, Georgia 3
Col. George V. Millett, Jr., Commanding Officer
   of 507th Parachute Infantry 5
507th Parachute Infantry Motor Pool; 5
Fred Peschl after completion of parachute training 9
Fred Peschl completes his ninth jump
   in Alliance, Nebraska 12
Fred Peschl completes jump
   in Denver, July 13, 1943 14
Father (Capt.) John J. Verret,
   Catholic Chaplain 507th Parachute Infantry 5
Fred Peschl at Tollerton Hall,
   Nottingham, England, June 1944 17
Preparing to jump on D-Day 25
Paratroopers jumping from airplane 27
Line drawing of Stalag Luft IV 38
Hand drawing of POWs' room at Stalag Luft IV
   by Howard Farr 39
Hand drawing of Marcy Peschl by Gordon Fisher 41
Hand drawing that shows the delivery of
   Red Cross packages by Howard Farr 43
Hand drawing of the Blessed Virgin Mary 45
Cartoon of Thanksgiving dinner at Stalag Luft IV 47
Hand drawing of a Kreige room at Stalag Luft IV
   ready for the holiday season by Howard Farr 48

Hand drawing of a Kreige room at Stalag Luft IV
   by Howard Farr 49
Fred Peschl and friends by
   guard tower at Stalag 357 55
Fred Peschl with chickens and Howard Farr 56
Fred Peschl and Howard Farr at Stalag 357 57

List of Maps

Map 1   Transportation of prisoners from Amfreville,
   France to Stalag Luft IV, Gross Tychow 62
Map 2.   The "Long March" from Stalag Luft IV to
   Stalag 357, Fallingbostel, Germany 83

Acknowledgments

Many people have played an important part in my life. Without them, this book would not have been possible. I want to thank Howard Farr and Art Schwegert for their friendship ever since we met in Stalag Luft IV. We helped each other survive the prison camp and the long, brutal march to Stalag 357 and 11-B. We've been friends ever since.

I want to thank Father John Verret for his pastoral support all the way from the 507th Parachute Infantry Jump School until D-Day. He and Joe Poplawski wrote to Marcie after they found out I was a prisoner-of-war. Father Lynch gave us hope and encouragement in the prison camp. Monsignor Carlton Hermann has been both a good friend and pastor ever since he was the priest at St. Thomas Aquinas Catholic Church in DeSmet, South Dakota. Fr. Cathal Gallagher, currently serving St. Thomas Aquinas Catholic Church, provided editorial comments on this book. My faith was important in helping me through life, and I owe much of that faith to these men.

The people of DeSmet have been important to me and my family. I want to thank those who supported my meat business and those who worked for me at the butcher shop and store. Thanks to those with whom I've worked across the country in the meat equipment business.

Finally, I wish to thank my family for all they've meant to me through the years. My wife, Marcie, wrote to me almost every day when I was in Ireland and England and when I was in Stalag 357. I looked forward to her letters more than anything. I thank my children, Terry and Vicki, their spouses, Dianne Peschl and Tom Artzner, and my grandchildren, Amy Peschl, Meesha Artzner, and Andy

Artzner, for making life so good. Each has been an important chapter in the book of my life.

> Fred Peschl
> DeSmet, South Dakota
> May 6, 1999

Introduction

I've known Fred Peschl since I was a teenager attending high school in DeSmet, South Dakota. Fred and his family attended nearly all of the school's functions. He was a big supporter of DeSmet High School athletics. Fred operated the meat market where we bought our meat. And we attended the same church, St. Thomas Aquinas Catholic Church. Fred was an active part of the community and was known by nearly everyone in town.

Most of us knew that Fred had been a prisoner of war (POW) in Germany during World War II, although he rarely spoke of it. We'd ask Fred to tell us about his experiences, but he was reluctant to do so. Having been in the service myself, I was always curious about Fred's experiences. In December 1997, Fred was having breakfast at the local cafe – something he and a group of other men in the community do nearly every morning. Fred started to tell the story of his time as a POW. Those who heard Fred that morning said they were fascinated by the story, which last almost two hours. Fred told them that he really hadn't told the whole story to anyone before that morning, not even to his own family. He said that he felt the need to tell the story and get it written down. My father, Dale Goreham, told Fred that, as sociologist, I collect these kinds of stories.

Fred contacted me a few weeks later and we set up a time for him to tell his story. We met on March 18, 1998 at his store, at the kitchen table in his house, and in his basement. I audio tape-recorded Fred's story for eight hours. I transcribed the recordings and asked Fred to check the transcriptions. The material in the transcriptions, along with other materials that Fred collected (see Additional References section), were used to write his story. Some of the material in the transcriptions was reordered into chronological order for easier reading, although every effort was taken to keep "Fred's voice" in this book.

Each person has a couple of events that happen during their lives that define and shape who they are. These defining events become the backdrop that directs us in our lives. For some people, it is an era like the Great Depression; for others, it is a religious conversion; for others, it is accomplishing a goal. For Fred, being a POW during World War II became one of his defining events.

Fred and I laughed together and cried together as he told his story. As you read this book, you are entering into something very sacred – the heart and soul of a man. I wish to extend my thanks to Fred for sharing his life with us.

> Gary A. Goreham, Ph.D.
> Department of Sociology/Anthropology
> North Dakota State University, Fargo
> June 1999

1. Paratrooper Training

My story began in a small South Dakota town. I was born in Yankton on May 24th, 1919 to John and Mary Peschl. I went to grade school at Sacred Heart Catholic School, and graduated from Yankton Public High School in 1938. Right away I started working for John Marek at the Standard Meat Market. He came from Czechoslovakia with my dad – that's how I knew him.

* * * * *

I worked for Lawrence Welk in Yankton. I ran my Model-T around for him. He only lived two blocks from our place near the hospital. Once I said to him, "Lawrence, I want 15¢ an hour for Jim, 15¢ for Joe, and 15¢ for me. I don't care how many hours we work. That's what I want."

But he kept paying me in Honolulu fruit gum. I said, "Lawrence, I don't want any more gum. I can't buy gas, and gas is 15¢ a gallon."

He said, "You don't want any more gum?"

"I don't care how much gum you got, I don't want any more," I said. "If you don't give me the 15¢, I quit."

So he said, "I'll pay you the money then. I want you to shovel the walk and cut the grass and do like you're doing. You do a good job."

I gave him more than a good job. I was just barely out of high school, or maybe still in high school. We got that straightened out with him. I also worked for some doctors in town. They all paid me 15¢ an hour. Every once in a while they gave me a nickel, a dime, or a quarter tip. Lawrence never gave me a money tip, but he gave me a gum tip.

* * * * *

The war came along a few years later. I figured I had to go to the service and I wanted to join the Navy. My friends and I thought that would be the way to go. I tried to join the Navy, but I couldn't get in because of my eyes, so I stayed home for a couple of years. I worked at the Standard Meat Market as a butcher and drove to neighboring towns to sell meat and sausage from the truck for $18 a week.

I married Marcella Schmidt on September 23, 1941 in Yankton. Marcie and her parents lived on a farm near the little town of Menominee, Nebraska, just across the river from Yankton. Every time I went to see her, it cost me 50¢ to cross the bridge on the Missouri River; it cost a dime for a passenger. That's what I did with that Model-T. I drove back and forth.

I got a draft card in January or February of 1942. There was no problem with my eyes for getting into the Army! We took the bus to Omaha, Nebraska to be sworn in on May 6, 1942. Before we left Yankton, we met at the College Café. That was quite a surprise because it was the first time I'd eaten breakfast away from home. We arrived in Omaha and were sworn in at 11:30 that night. The next morning we got on a train to go to Manhattan, Kansas and wait for our orders. When our orders arrived, they told us where we were going and what we were going to do in the service. They give us some tests to see what we wanted to do. Since I worked in the meat market, I was supposed to go to Cook School at Camp Walters in Mineral Wells, Texas.

When I got to Mineral Wells, there was a big sign across the street that said this was the home of Judy Garland, the movie star. Basic training lasted 13 weeks. It was a lot tougher than I thought it would be. Marcie was with me when I went to Cook School. The toughest thing for her was when I was at Camp Walters, which is between Fort Worth and Dallas. Neither Marcie nor I had been that far away from home. I went through Cook School and Basic Training at the same time at Camp Walters. During Basic

Training, we went into the Sand Hills on maneuvers. We had bivouac and slept in pup tents. They give us quite a bit of training that way.

We were put on a troop train in August 1942. I didn't know where we were going, and neither did anyone else. We just knew that we were going east. One fellow on the train was named Rice. He had been in cook school with me. He had no intentions of being a parachute jumper. I knew that. He was older than I by maybe about 15 or 20 years, twice as old as I was. He brought all the lemon and vanilla extract out of the kitchen with him. He drank it all the way to Georgia because it had alcohol in it. He got sicker and drunker than hell on it. I didn't know you could get that drunk on that stuff. He drank bottle after bottle.

* * * * *

We got to Georgia and went to Fort Benning. I had no idea why we were there or what we were going to do. At first we weren't doing anything. As the Regiment got organized, they needed cooks and the motor pool so we were the very first ones there. We were in what was called the "Frying Pan" area. It was in west central Georgia near the Chattahoochee River across from Alabama. It was real hot there, sultry hot.

We weren't doing much of anything in the barracks and one day Colonel George Millett, commanding officer of the 507th Parachute Infantry, asked for a bunch of us guys to come to his headquarters. We were "gold bricking," and that's exactly what we were doing – nothing. We came to his headquarters, a square tent with a wooden floor. We stood in front the Colonel and the other officers – Capt. James Dickerson, Maj. Ben Pearson, Capt. William Miller, Lt. Col. Arthur Malony, Maj. Gordon Smith, and Sgt. Fitzpatrick. They were all standing.

Col. Millet said, "Soldier, come up here." He was looking at all eight or ten of us. "Yes, you," he said, looking right at me.

507th Parachute Infantry training at Ft. Benning, Georgia

"OK," I said, and walked part way up to him and saluted.

He asked, "What's your name?"

"P-P-P-Peschl," I stuttered.

"Can't you talk?" he asked.

"Yes, sir. Peschl."

He asked, "Do you want to be my driver?"

"I guess so."

"Do you or don't you?"

I said, "Yes, sir!"

"OK, come up here and see the sergeant. You go with him and get a jeep. Keep the jeep for the rest of the next three days. Drive all over Fort Benning and figure out where you're going and where the people I want to see everyday are. You come back to my quarters at 5:30 in the morning on Monday. We'll go down to the field and watch them jump."

So I went with the sergeant and did everything he told me. I drove around all over. It was just like going to a big city. I couldn't believe how big that was. I got lost many times, but I found my way around.

I drove down to pick up the Colonel every morning for the next couple weeks. We'd go down and watch part of the cadre coming into our paratroop regiment, the 507th, or into other paratroop regiments. There were about 800 men who started every week. That number dropped to 400 or 450 who made it through Parachute School. The other ones washed out. I had no intention of being in the paratroops – I came to cook.

We went along like that for a couple of weeks. Then the Colonel asked me, "Would you like to be my permanent driver?

I said, "I would like to be."

Col. George V. Millett, Jr., Commanding Officer of 507th Parachute Infantry (Source: *507th Parachute Infantry: 1943*)

"Well, you would have to go to Parachute School," he said, "and you'll get $50 a month more."

I was getting $21 a month at the time, but I thought that $50 a month was a pretty good deal. I said, "I'd really like that extra $50 a month, but I don't know about the jumping." I asked him if I could just jump once and see if I liked it.

He said, "No, don't even think about it. You'd have to go to school just like the rest of them."

"I'll have to think about it," I told him. Now I had never even flown before. About the first airplane I ever flew in, I jumped out of. I flew in a little airplane in Yankton once, but otherwise I never had an airplane ride.

Marcie, my wife, had come with me to Fort Benning. She was staying with a Major's family at the Fort and worked for him. I didn't dare to tell her I was thinking about going to Parachute School. I thought I'd just sign up for the next class when it started. I was in school the next week.

Marcie could see when the men were up on the tower, but she didn't know I was in the training for almost two weeks. I was on the towers the third week. Everyday she said she could watch those guys jumping.

Finally I told her, "You watch next week because I'll be on the towers." That was the first time she knew I was in there.

"What are you doing that for?" she asked, "Why did you do that?"

"I wanted to be the Colonel's driver and I wanted the $50 a month," I answered.

"Well, are you sure you want that?"

I said, "Yes, I am now because I'm part way through. I don't plan to quit. I just made up my mind and I'm determined to do it."

She didn't cry or say she was going home or anything.

507th Parachute Infantry Motor Pool; T/5 Fred L. Peschl (second row; fifth from left)
(Source: *507th Parachute Infantry: 1943*)

She didn't know what to say. She was just dumbfounded. And that's the way that was. She thought it was just awful the way the men had to drop off of that tower.

I told her, "It's not as bad on the tower as it looks. You know they're going to catch you because they haven't dropped anybody yet, I guess. But it sure scares everything out of you."

* * * * *

I tasted olives with red pimentos for the first time ever because I drove the Colonel around. I drove him to a restaurant once in Atlanta, Georgia. Later, when we were in Alliance, Nebraska, I drove him over to Denver and he'd spend the weekend there. He'd always take different ones of his officers with him. I always got a hotel room and he gave me money to spend while I was there. He was always real good to me, and I was good to him, too. He said, "Be here at 6 o'clock to pick me up," and I was there at 6 o'clock.

* * * * *

One morning during the week just before I started Parachute School, the Colonel and I went down to watch the cadre do their jumps, just like we did every morning. There were some Canadian officers who were going to Parachute School with the enlisted men. The officers and enlisted men weren't treated differently when they were in Parachute School. We didn't even know that someone was an officer unless he told you. He was the same as us – just another GI. As these Canadians were going do their jumps, the planes came in at the same height. The ones in the back should have been up higher. When the men in the front airplanes jumped out, the planes in the back were too low. The canopies of men's parachutes floated into the planes right behind them. Some of them caught on the wings, and some got into the propellers. Those that caught on the wings just stayed there and their bodies were like toothpicks. They flew right up and hit the fuselage or the wing. Some of their bodies dropped right to the ground. All of them dropped someplace, but some of them dropped to the ground right away. We were standing close to where they were coming down. One body hit very close to us. You could see the bodies coming down like long pencils turning over and over. They didn't come down head first or feet first, but just turned. When their bodies hit the ground, they hit on the side, the face, the back, or whatever. They went right into the ground. It made an indentation in that hard ground, the same ground the planes took off from. There were about five who were killed out of that group. That's what I had that to think about as I started Parachute School the following week!

* * * * *

I managed to get through all four weeks of training. Every morning we started to train at 5:00. We got up, ran, did double time, had breakfast around 6:30, then had more training. We did calisthenics during much of the morning – push ups! During the afternoons we learned how to pack our own chutes. We had to stand at attention practically all the time. Even if we were sweaty, we couldn't move our hands from our sides.

If I moved my hands, they'd say, "Peschl, give me 10 push ups as fast as you can!" They'd say, "Give me 20 push ups!" if I just tried to wipe a fly off of my nose.

We couldn't do anything with our hands or move our feet. We just had to stand at attention when we stopped doing calisthenics. That's the way it was. Those sergeants were good. They were trained. The jump master sergeant in the plane told us he was tough, too.

There were no colored people in our outfit. They never had them in there in those days. Everybody went in for the same reason, but they would wash out about half of them every time. I was surprised at that. We'd see a guy one day, and the next day we didn't see him. Guys got washed out if they didn't do some of the things they were told. Some of them wouldn't go on the towers. They just refused. Maybe they went one whole day and ran and ran and ran until they just dropped. Then they did calisthenics until they dropped.

They told us to do all those things and we did them the way they told us. Otherwise, they said, "We're going to boot you." If they kicked someone out – they were out. If they dropped out or said, "No, I'm not going to do it." – they were done. Once someone said, "No," they were done right at that point. They just walked away. A lot of men thought about it one or maybe two nights, then we wouldn't see them the third day. They thought about it all night and they thought they couldn't do it any more the next day. They went back to where they came from. Maybe some of them came all the way from California to go to Parachute School. Where they went then, I don't know. They were just done as far as Parachute School goes.

The third week we had to jump off the towers. Everybody dreaded the thought of it, but we knew we had to do it. I made five jumps in parachute school – one everyday for five days. We usually got up around 5:00 in the morning and made the jumps between 6:00 and 8:00. Joe Poplawski, a short Polish man from Pennsylvania, and I made the jumps together. We were always together. We'd jump either third or fourth. We changed around a little bit, but we always knew we wanted to be together if we could. Joe and I were excited when we got through Parachute School.

* * * * *

Here's how to use the parachute. The main thing is to land on your feet. There are many risers, maybe 72 of them – silk strings going up to the parachute. Of course that was all silk, too. There were two main risers on either side of the parachute. You take two risers in your right hand and two in your left hand. Then, just before you think you're going to hit the ground, you had to pull real hard. It brings you up, and the parachute down. It slows you down enough so you don't hit the ground too hard. If the silk comes right down over the top of you it's a really good landing. You can almost stand up that way. You're coming down real nice and you see the land out there and you think, "Oh, that's nice." You think that the ground is down further, but it's right here. If you hit it hard and your legs are straight, you can break both legs. I never felt like I hit the ground. I always felt like the ground came up and hit me. The ground will hit you faster than you think. It's more sudden than you expect. You can see yourself coming down and everything seems OK. You're floating really nice, but you don't realize how fast you're coming until you hit that ground. That's when it fools you.

You don't want your feet real straight, just let them stay limber. Let your knees bend, then roll with it if you can. If your knees bend and you hit light, you'll almost stand up. But the best thing is to roll because you get your weight off your legs. When you hit the ground, you should make a tumble. If you don't make that tumble, you can get hurt. That's what they taught us in Parachute School all the time, and that's why we did calisthenics all the time. I just happened to land good, not that I always did it right or anything. I just landed luckily.

The wind can oscillate you and you can come down and hit on your side. The wind is going to make you oscillate no matter what. I don't know if there's a way to stop oscillating or not unless you can pull on two risers and hold yourself up. During oscillation, you may never get a chance to pull on the risers. If you know how to control the chute a little bit, you can pull the two risers and go one way, then pull the other two risers. You should have both hands on two risers. Just before you think you're going to hit the ground, pull hard on them. That brings you up just a little bit so you touch the ground easier.

A streamer is when you jump and your chute comes

out of the package, but doesn't blossom. There's no way you can control it or do anything except hit the ground. If you hit the ground that fast, it'll kill you.

Our chutes were all opened by a static line. There were 11 to 15 men on either side of the "stick" or line of men in the airplane. One man jumps out of the airplane door from one side, then another man goes from the other side – every other guy. Another way is when one whole line stands up on one side and hooks up to the line. Then the other line stands up behind them. They all start to crowd toward the door. I always liked to be close to the door to jump out first instead of last. The Jump Master was up in the front of the airplane and would stand up. He'd push you out if you didn't go. If you acted like you were going to go straight ahead past the door, he'd make sure he stopped you and pushed you out. Even if you got pushed out, your chute opened anyway.

The airplanes flew at about 500 feet when you jumped out. In combat, you'd jump out at 400 feet or less. The closer they flew to the ground, the better because then they didn't have a chance to shoot at you as long. But, it's harder on the planes because they're so low. They've got to get out of the way of the flack. The flack goes right on past the airplane. You can see it, but it doesn't burst until it gets up higher. Although if the flack goes through the plane, you're a goner.

* * * * *

I never saw the Colonel during the time I was in parachute training, but I knew he was checking on me to see how I was doing. I didn't see him around at all, but I saw his jeep drive by from time to time. I got through Parachute School and was able to get an eight-day furlough. I was excited about going home for a few days. Marcie and I took a train back to South Dakota. I remember walking up and down the street at Yankton with my paratrooper boots on. People couldn't believe that I would have done that. I said

I couldn't believe it either! We went back to Fort Benning and finished the training. Then, I drove the Colonel's jeep.

The 507th Regiment was activated on July 20th, 1942. The regiment went across the Chatahoochie River from Fort Benning, Georgia to Alabama after Christmas. We trained there until March 7th, 1943. We had a big Christmas party

Fred Peschl after completion of parachute training

outside because the weather was so nice. There were many things to eat. We could invite our wives, girlfriends, or whoever was there. We enjoyed that a lot.

As we were going to the Frying Pan in Alabama, we went through Columbus, Georgia. We had to cross the Chatahoochie River on a cable ferry. It wasn't so much of a ferry as it was a flat barge that crossed the river on a cable. If we didn't get there before 1:00, they tied it up with a chain to the side of the river because it was Sunday. We missed the ferry after it crossed over the river for the last time of the day. Some of the men who were half drunk got there after 1:00 and tried to cross the river on the cable. They got out half way and fell into the river, and it was deep. Still, some more of them kept trying to cross the river that way. Joe Poplawski and I were on a bridge that crossed the river. We were both looking down at the water and talking about the next parachute jump we were going to make. Joe said, "Fred, I don't know if I can jump tomorrow or not. Look at how far it is down to the river!"

Not everybody made that jump at the same time, but I had to make it. That was my toughest jump – that sixth jump. Joe Poplawski didn't make the jump with me because he went on maneuvers. So I made the sixth one without him. I dreaded making that jump so soon after the first five at parachute school. I don't know what it was about that sixth jump, but I just dreaded it. I couldn't sleep the night before that jump. I thought about it all the time. After that, I felt better about the jumps I made and didn't think about them nearly as much.

* * * * *

Marcie and I, two guys, and another little gal were asked by a GI friend to go to Miami, Florida and be together after Christmas. He didn't have a girlfriend or wife. We thought that would be great. The Colonel let me go between Christmas and New Years. My friend had a station wagon.

Fred Peschl completes his ninth jump at Alliance, Nebraska.

Instead of saying, "I'm going to drive my car home," he'd say, "I'm going to carry my car home." I don't know where he got that brogue.

We went to Miami and stayed in someone's home. I'd never been in Florida, so we went all the way down to Key West and the whole bit. There were other soldiers with us and other women we met when we got down there. The soldiers were drinking rum and Coca Cola, but I wanted to go to the Orange Bowl football game instead. It was just a few blocks away – not very far. Boston College was playing Alabama. I got over there and stood outside the gate of the Orange Bowl stadium in uniform watching people go in, but I didn't have a ticket.

An officer came up to me, and I said, "Hello, Colonel."

He said, "Hello, soldier. Would you like to go to the game?"

"Yes, sir," I said, "I sure would."

"Come on, and we'll go in," he said, "My wife didn't want to go. I'd just as soon take you." So he took me in.

We sat four rows back on the 50 yard line and saw the whole game. He bought me a hotdog and hamburger and some other things to eat. I got a program for 25¢. He was very nice and I enjoyed the game. He asked me all about jumping and everything. I hadn't done it very long, just through October, November, and December. After the game was over, the colonel offered to take me back to where I was staying.

I said, "I've got a ways to walk to where I'm staying."

He said, "Oh, I'll take you back."

I said, "I don't even know the address, but I know about where the place is." So he took me home, then he went home. I don't even know what kind of officer he was anymore. How could I have been so lucky? It was really something that I got to go to that game at that time. I'd never been away from home, you might say. That colonel just saw me standing there all alone. I was lucky that I was alone and had my uniform on. If I hadn't he probably wouldn't have asked me. He was going to take somebody. He stayed right there and wanted to know if I wanted a ride home and everything.

* * * * *

Fred Peschl completes jump in Denver, July 3, 1943

    The regiment returned to Fort Benning in mid-January 1943. We were there only a short time when we found out that we were to go on maneuvers at Barksdale Field, Louisiana near Shreveport. That was on March 7th, 1943. From there we went to Alliance Air Base, Alliance, Nebraska. Marcie came with me to Nebraska. I didn't know where Alliance was except that it was south of the Black Hills in South Dakota.

The Colonel asked me if I would drive his staff car up to Alliance while the others came by train. I said that would be just great. I asked if I could take Marcie home to Yankton. He said that would be fine. Yankton wasn't many miles out of the way. I thought it would be a good time to be home for a while after Christmas. So Marcie and I drove to Yankton while they went on maneuvers. The maneuvers went alright and no one got hurt. The regiment arrived on March 20th, 1943.

Two or three weeks after the regiment arrived in Alliance, there were several of us who had to make a jump. I was one of them. That was to be my seventh jump. The day we were supposed to jump was very windy. There was so much wind and dust on the ground that we just landed without jumping. We were glad to have landed because it was too dangerous and too many of us could have gotten hurt. We went up a few days later and made the jump.

* * * * *

The only maneuvers I went on were up in South Dakota, although some of the men went on maneuvers in Louisiana before coming to Nebraska. One whole Company flew in airplanes from Fort Benning over to Louisiana and jumped. Not all of the men would have jumped because some of them took the trucks and drove to Louisiana to pick up the chutes. The riggers packed the chutes and took care of them. We were taught how to pack our own chutes during school, but all the rest of the chutes were packed by the riggers. A good friend of mine was a rigger. He and his wife lived in the same little motel as Marcie and I when we were in Alliance. We were together because his wife was there, too. I didn't do anything on those maneuvers down in Louisiana. I missed all that by driving the Colonel's car back to South Dakota and then to Alliance. I was in Alliance before the regiment arrived. I wanted to be sure I was there when the Colonel got there. I was, too, because when he said, "Jump!," I jumped.

When we were in practice out in Alliance, they would fly over a lake and make a water landing. I knew I never wanted to do that, and the Colonel knew I didn't want to. He said, "If we have to make a water landing for the war, we'll do it then." But some guys volunteered to make a water landing. There was a small lake they found to use for the jump. Two plane loads went up with 40 guys in each plane. They jumped out into the water. In water landings, you come down real nice and set right down in that water. But, if you let the chute set on top of you, it will smother you. You can't get out around it. We lost five guys in that water landing in Nebraska because they drowned. Their chutes landed right over the top of them and the silk smothered them. They couldn't get air and couldn't get out of their chutes in the water. We didn't make anymore water landings after that.

There were others who got killed during training. I went to about 10 funerals a month for guys who had streamers or who drowned in the water. It was just awful there for a while. If you thought about it, you just couldn't get it out of your mind. Those who got hurt bad were out of the paratroops – maybe even out of the service for all we knew. Some of them got healed up and were put in another outfit someplace. There was always a place for them somewhere. I don't know where any of those men went.

* * * * *

We trained in Alliance all of summer and fall of 1943. Some of the guys went hunting for pheasants out there. We went fishing on Sundays or on days off.

Each company trained in Alliance with different kinds of weapons, like bazookas and mortars. My job was to get the Colonel from one company to another, over here and over there, back and forth, to meetings and to things like that. So I missed that part of the weapons training. But I did have to make those jumps, like the big jump at the Denver Municipal Airport.

The jump in Denver was supposed to be a big deal. We were to "take the airport" on July 3rd, 1943. Over 150,000 people came out to watch it. They had to sign their name and give a pint of blood at the Red Cross Mobile Unit. That's what the exercise was originally for. One group of men was to move against the airport's north gate, and a second group moved to the center of the airport. A third group went to the south gate to circle the airport. About 250 of us had to make the jump in Denver. I always jumped with some Company, but not necessarily with the Colonel. I had to make the jump, and I think he made that one, too.

A lot of guys landed hard because the air was so light. There were so many cars out there in Denver with all those thousands of people. Some guys came down and straddled both legs over the hood of one of the cars and broke both legs. There were over 80 broken bones that day. I couldn't believe how many got hurt out there because of that light air. We left Denver with 73 out of 300 guys in Fitzsimons General Hospital, which you could see from the airport. They had broken legs, broken arms, hurt backs, or something like that from that landing. It was terrible. They never jumped again.

I was fortunate that I wasn't hurt in that jump. On my way down, I was oscillating quite a bit because the wind was blowing and the air was light and came down faster than hell. I was oscillating and didn't know it. If you oscillate and hit the ground, it'll hurt like hell. That's the way I came down at the airport in Denver. I landed on the runway on my side. I really landed hard on the ground – terribly hard. I was sore for quite a few days. I was lucky that I could even walk. That was the hardest landing I ever made. I was scared with that one, but it was a good enough landing. That was my eighth jump.

I made two jumps in Alliance and one in South Dakota – my tenth one. We went on maneuvers October 19th, 1943 at Stockade Lake, Custer State Park, South Dakota. During those maneuvers, I made a jump at Custer State Park. We bivouacked in the park and were there for Thanksgiving. All the guys had a big time up there. They shot deer and pheasants and anything they could see. They weren't supposed to – I knew that – but they did. We had feeds and bonfires out there. We cooked the deer, fish, and everything. We got orders that we were going overseas while we were up there. So we gathered up everything we had and went back to Alliance to say farewell to everybody there.

The Colonel let me go for two or three days to take Marcie home. She was pregnant at the time. I left my car home and hitchhiked back. It was pouring rain while I was hitchhiking and I got soaking wet out there on the highway. When I got back, it wasn't long before we were put on two troop trains. One train went north through Montana and Canada and came down at Buffalo, New York, then on to Camp Shanks, New York. The other train went south through Nebraska and east until it ended up at Camp Shanks, which was right near New York City.

Camp Shanks was up the river a little way from West Point on the Hudson River. I never went to West Point although some of the guys got up there and looked at it. I went to New York City a few times while I was there. We had to take a ferry and cross Staten Island or Manhattan Island. We got shots there to go overseas. That was awful. I don't know how many shots we had – it seemed like 10 or 15. Some of them were just horrible. They made me so sick that I was just terribly sick for days. I was glad to go to New York once or twice because I never thought I'd ever make it back there again because I was so sick.

In New York City, we went to Madison Square Garden to see some boxing. We saw the polo grounds,

Brooklyn Park, and Brooklyn Stadium. The polo grounds are way down low. We had to be way up high on the highway or on the road and see the polo grounds down below. We saw Yankee Stadium, but there were no ball games in December. I went downtown a couple of times to look at the big buildings. I had never been in New York City before. They had a big orchestra like the Blue Baron or Guy Lombardo playing music for the soldiers while we were at the camp. That was a big deal then. I never went to watch any of them, although I did hear them. I didn't feel like doing any dancing.

    We never knew when we were going overseas. We figured we were going to get on a ship soon, but we didn't know when, where, or what kind of ship. They didn't tell us anything. No one got any mail. When our son, Terry, was born, I didn't get any mail telling that he had been born. He was born on December 2nd, 1943, and we left on the 6th. I got on the boat on the 4th, and left the harbor on the 6th. I'm sure the telegram that told me about Terry's birth was on the boat with us in the mail someplace. We were in the harbor a couple of days getting loaded after we got on the boat. There was probably two or three times as many men as should have been on the boat.

    Our ship was called the Stratenaver. It was an old English transport ship, which I was told had been built way back in the 1880s. I was in F-Deck, six flights down. It was very stuffy. I couldn't stand it down there, so I came up and I stayed on top. I didn't want anything to eat. I had been sick from the shots back at the camp, but had gotten over that to some extent.

    We started out in a ship convoy from the New York harbor on December 6th, 1943 and went up toward the New England states, Newfoundland, and across to Iceland. There were icebergs out there in December.

    All the way over I was sick every day. I went up on the deck and found a rope with a life saver tied to it. I got inside of that thing and tied the rope to the deck so I wouldn't roll off. The boat turned and rolled, as big as it was. I felt like a cork out there sometimes. I just slept out there all the way over there as much as I could. It was cold and foggy. I couldn't see my hand in front of me sometimes. We could hear the fog horns blowing all the time. Once in a while someone would shout, "Submarine!" or "Iceberg!" I never saw anything, but I wondered what was out there. Sometimes I'd go inside and watch the men gamble. There were stairs going up one way and stairs going up another way and they'd be down there gambling. Money was all over the floor. We landed in Liverpool, England on December 15th, 1943.

* * * * *

2. Preparing for D-Day

Our transport ship, the Stratenaver, was so huge that it couldn't land in Ireland, so we landed in Liverpool, England on December 15th, 1943. The first thing I noticed in Liverpool was a sign for John Morrell & Company. I was in the meat business so I would notice John Morrell from Sioux Falls, South Dakota. I really started being impressed by the Red Cross while I was in Liverpool. They had coffee and donuts for us when we arrived.

We could get off the ship, but we had to stay on the deck that night. The next day, we got on the American liberty ship Susan B. Anthony with our GI duffle bags. The liberty ships were much smaller than the Stratenaver had been, but they were good ships. They took us across the Irish Sea. It was a horrible ride, as rough as a cob. I was terribly sea sick – a lot of us were. I couldn't eat or do anything. Many times I've thought how good it was that I didn't get in the Navy since I got so sea sick. I'd have been sick all the time. I liked to be on the land.

We carried our duffle bags, but we never had our weapons or our parachutes with us. We had everything we owned in those duffle bags. If we wanted anything at all, it was in our duffle bags or on us. If we had a picture of somebody, a prayer book, or things like that, we had to carry it with us. We couldn't have anything big because we just didn't want to carry that much.

The trip on the liberty ship took a couple of days and nights to cross the Irish Sea. We arrived in Belfast on December 22nd, 1943. It was another day before we got unloaded. I don't know how many went besides us in the 507th, but I know there were about 2,500 of us. After we arrived in Belfast, we were supposed to go in trucks to our camp. We had to wait a long time for the trucks. They took us to the town of Portrush, which was cold and windy because it is on the northern tip of Ireland. We got there just before Christmas. We could see the sea from where we were at Portrush. It was cold, wet, and miserable.

We drove up to the billets at Portrush in the trucks, and jumped out to see what we were getting into. There was a big load of hay there – just plain, old hay. They gave us big, long gunny sacks and said, "Fill them up however you want. That's your bed." After stuffing hay into the gunny sacks, we went in the billets to find a place to sleep for the night. It was already late at night, perhaps almost midnight.

Someone said, "Just find a place to sleep for tonight and tomorrow night. If you want to sleep with somebody different in a room, we'll figure that out later." I walked up two or three flights of stairs and stopped. I saw a room with somebody in it already. It looked like there was room so I went in. I ended up with somebody else that I knew later on. We stayed there a few days and then sorted out according to companies, and I went to a different building.

We were training while we were at Portrush. One thing we knew we weren't going to get at Portrush was another jump. We couldn't make our jumps because it was too cold, windy, and wet during December. Most of the GIs in our outfit had ground training everyday, like walking around with gas masks on. We trained everyday even though we weren't going to make a jump. We knew we had to make a jump sometime – a night jump before we went to wherever it was we were going.

We didn't know where we were going or anything. We were at Portrush just to be someplace and to wait for whatever was coming – D-Day, I guess. We never heard the word "D-Day" until after it happened. We were just waiting for a day, and it ended up being called D-Day

When we were in Ireland, the sick and wounded

paratroopers of the 508th arrived. They had jumped with General Gavin in Sicily and Italy. They were in hospitals in Northern Ireland in the same area as we were. A lot of them were in the hospital with all kinds of sickness. Some called it "Chinese rock" or "syph." They were loaded with it. We were warned to stay away from anyone who might carry it. That's what we were told right away.

* * * * *

When we arrived in Ireland, the mail was sorted. I had a telegram in the mail from Marcie. It was dated 11:43 a.m. on December 2nd, 1943, and read:

> CPL FRED PESCHL 37123918 SERVICE CO
> 507TH PARACHUTE INFANTRY APO
> 9030 CARE
> POSTMASTER NYK
> SON BORN. SEVEN POUNDS. ALL WELL. CAN YOU COME?
> MARCELLA

* * * * *

I wondered why the Colonel picked me to be his driver. I saw the Colonel in Portrush one day and I didn't need to drive him any place.

I asked, "Say, Colonel, you know, I've always wondered. Why did you pick me back in Georgia to be your driver?"

He said, "You were the only one who had clean coveralls on." We were all just goldbricking, doing nothing. The others were drivers from the motor pool. I was the cook. He knew that later, but not at first. He didn't know why I was there. He just knew that we were goldbricking.

* * * * *

Father (Capt.) John Verret was with us from the very beginning at Fort Benning. He wrote the motto for the 507th Parachute Infantry – *Descende Ad Terram*, which means

"Down to Earth." He was with us in Nebraska and Ireland. Father Verret had places to go, and wondered if I could take him in the jeep.

I said, "If you ask the Colonel, and it's OK, I'd be glad to drive you around, Father." So he did. I often took him different places to say Mass for other GIs. Most of the places we went to were near Portrush or the local air base.

Portrush was in Northern Ireland and we knew we had to stay in Northern Ireland. We were told to stay out of southern Ireland. The English owned Northern Ireland. We were there because things were too crowded in England. Northern Ireland isn't very big. The Colonel told me that if

Father (Capt.) John J. Verret, Catholic Chaplain 507th **Parachute Infantry** (Source: *507*[th] *Parachute Infantry: 1943*)

I drove the jeep anywhere or took Father Verret someplace to say Mass, that I should never go into the other part of Ireland.

He said, "We could never get you out. There's no way I could get you out. If you get over there and you're stuck, then you're stuck." I always paid attention as to where I was with the jeep.

One day I drove Father Verret to say Mass in a tent, which he almost always did. I usually sat in the back of the tent in case I had to go out. During church, I noticed some nurses in the front. I thought I should know one of them. When she came back from Communion, I recognized her. She was Dolores Dilger from Yankton, South Dakota who was in my class at Sacred Heart School and in high school. I couldn't believe it. Her dad was a dentist in Yankton. He pulled a couple of my teeth when I was a kid. I waited until I went to Communion, then I nodded to her and said, "Hi." I shook hands with her right then and there.

She said, "I'll see you right after Mass."

I went back and sat in my pew. After Mass I went up to her and had a nice visit. She told me that when the planes went to France, Holland, Bastogne, or wherever, her job was to help bring back the wounded. She would be in with the paratroops, and would bring wounded paratroops back. If planes carrying troops to France could land, they'd return to England with the wounded. Of course the planes couldn't land the night when we jumped, but as we progressed the planes could land to pick up the wounded. That was going to be her job. It was such a surprise to see her there.

Do you know what she gave me? She handed me a fresh egg. She said, "You'd better take this egg to wherever you're living and have them fry it for you. You'll never get another one." That was a big thing. She handed me a fresh egg.

* * * * *

I never was an altar boy as I grew up in Yankton. I couldn't learn the prayers in Latin. I learned *ad Deum qui laetificat juventutem meam*, but that's all. That much took me a month to learn. If the prayers were in Bohemian, I could have learned them, but not Latin.

We were in Ireland at Christmas time. I remember going to Midnight Mass. Some of the other officers and GIs served Mass. Col. Maloney and Lt. Col. Ostberg both served Midnight Mass in Ireland when we heard some airplanes going over. There was a window in the church open just a bit. Somebody hurried to the window and shut it to block the light. Everything was dark in Ireland and England. They didn't want any lights on in the place. It was blacked out all the time.

German airplanes came over every once in a while. We never knew what they were going to do. We were aware of them all the time and talked about them. There weren't many guns on the ground in Ireland to shoot at the German airplanes. But in England, we saw the guns all the time. Anywhere we went, we could see guns, especially by the sea.

* * * * *

We were in Portrush, Ireland about three months – January, February, and March of 1944. Then we returned to England on liberty ships. We went to the northern part of England and got on trains and rode south. We saw the Queen Mary docked away from the coast. It was out on the water because they couldn't get into the harbor with the war conditions. We went down to Nottingham, which was north of London, and arrived at Tollerton Hall near Robin Hood Forest. Tollerton Hall was a big building made of cement and brick. That's were we set up our camp. We put up big, eight-man tents with wooden floors behind Tollerton Hall. The officers lived in the Hall and the enlisted men were out in the tents. It was a nice, quiet place.

They took a picture of us at Nottingham when we

where at Tollerton Hall. They picked enlisted guys from every state along with all of the officers. Col. Millet was in the front row of the picture, and so was the "Sherif of Nottingham." The Colonel asked me if I would come to represent South Dakota.

Plum Tree was a little town near Tollerton Hall. We could walk there because it was so close. I bought a bike and rode to Plum Tree whenever I wanted to until we left for the aerodrome just before D-day. We didn't know when it was coming or anything. We trained at Tollerton Hall, and we knew it wouldn't be long. We had a sense that something was coming, but didn't know what or where. We were on training and tried to make one jump. They wanted to make a night jump which we hadn't done yet. So we went out and lived in pup tents on a hill, two men in a tent. We waited for nicer weather to come because it was May of 1944, and it was cold. We slept in those tents for a solid week with water running through them. We had to wait for the jump to take place because it was raining and foggy. Finally, we made the night jump and landed in the mud. We didn't get hurt because we were up to our knees in mud. We were sopping wet and muddy. That was my eleventh jump.

*****

They gave us a big party on May 13th, 1944 at Tollerton Hall just before we jumped. It was a wild one – a three day deal. We could make it just as wild as we wanted to. The Colonel was good for parties. The party included field events, broad jump, high jump, track events, meals served at the mess hall, baseball, clowns, boxing, and a Red Cross show put on by "Four Jills without a Jeep." The main event was boxing with Pillboy Peen against Young Stripling. We had wrestling, squat drill competition, and silent drill. A bunch of guys came to the camp and furnished music. There was a dance that went from 8:30 p.m. to midnight. They invited as many women as wanted to come.

The party was about a month before D-day, so the Colonel knew it was going to be sometime in June. He went to London several times with his officers, but I wasn't allowed to go. They didn't want any passengers other than those who were going to the meeting. They didn't want to bother with anybody else or let them know about anything.

Fred Peschl at Tollerton Hall, Nottingham, England, June 1944

Sometime during the party, the Colonel got up and spoke. He said, "One of the things that you've got to face is that you might get killed. If you get wounded, we'll do the best we can to help you. But if you get taken prisoner, don't be a damned fool. If you get taken prisoner and think you can just walk away, get on a train, and go someplace, then you're thinking wrong. If you can speak German or French, then yes, maybe you can do that. But you're not going to do it just speaking English. If you get taken prisoner, it takes two of them to take care of you. So that's a real detriment to them. If they kill a whole bunch of you, we're going to kill a whole bunch of them. We'll show them it can be done both ways. But if you get taken prisoner, just don't make an ass out of yourself and think you can escape out of a railroad car or out of a barracks and not have a plan to make it all the way. If you don't think you can make it all the way, don't even try."

He told us that ahead of time. The main thing was that it takes two of them to take care of one of you. If they're back there taking care of you, they're not fighting against us. Of course they put the ones back there as guards that they didn't want on the front lines.

* * * * *

We weren't particularly afraid of what was going to happen. We heard about what the guys from the 508th were doing in Africa, Sicily, and part of Italy. It was just like hearing that a bunch of men jumped in Denver and many of them got hurt. We were just glad we hadn't done it, but we knew we were going to make the next jump in just two days or two weeks. We just did it.

We knew that some of us were going to get hurt or killed. We thought about it all the time. I thought about it so many times during those four days when I was on the ground after D-Day. The book, *The Longest Day*, explains it – everyday during the first five days was "the longest day" for me. There was one day right after the other, and each one seemed just as long.

Father Verret helped us make peace with what was going to happen. He talked about it many times in his sermons. Each person thought about it in his own mind a lot. I prayed a lot. I was never too smart in school, but I really did pray that I would come back and do the right thing. I prayed that I would always do the right thing in whatever I did. I prayed that I would enjoy what I did and feel good about it. Now I get up every morning and thank God that I'm here. I always say a little prayer: "I thank Thee, Almighty God, for all my thoughts, words, and actions of this day." No matter what I do, I thank Almighty God the minute I get up, walk out of the house, go to the bathroom, or get in the car to go to the store. Even though it isn't far between the house and the store, I thank God every single morning and make the sign of the cross, and maybe say the Hail Mary. I said oodles and oodles of Hail Marys. If I was saying them, I wouldn't go cookoo. I would just think about being home.

I never knew if I'd ever see Terry. I was one of the real fortunate ones. God picked me out. It's a lot like how the Colonel picked me out. I did everything he asked me to do and never questioned anything he said. I took him wherever he wanted to go. God brought me all the way back here.

* * * * *

There were runways nearby where we were sent to read the sand tables. Everyday they sent planes over to take pictures of the Normandy beaches to see where our positions would be. Our position was to be Amfreville, France. We were already at the aerodrome, but we never got near the planes. We just read the sand tables everyday, and everyday they were changed. But even then, they got it wrong where we actually were going to be. We thought we were going to Amfreville, but the German 91st Division was there. That's where I was taken prisoner. The German general was in a house on the farm right near Amfreville. They didn't know that he was moving in there, but he moved in there May 24th, 1944 with a whole Division. They knew about where a Panzer Division was, but they didn't expect him to be there. They were trying to do all of this thinking ahead of time so that they would know where everything was.

* * * * *

Shortly after my 11th jump, we were trucked to the aerodrome at Barkeston Heath. They put the bunks side by side real close together in the aerodrome. The bunk beds were so close that we could hardly walk between them. We had to push our knees between them to get in and lay down, unless we got in on an end bunk. There wasn't anything else in there – just men and bunks. They fed us very well in that aerodrome. We had orange juice, candy bars, fruit, and all kinds of things like that – things that we didn't get to eat otherwise. That's all we did. We ate good and slept.

One of our own units guarded us. We couldn't leave the building. We were guarded all the time so that none of us would leave or see anyone else except just each other. After a few days, some men shot themselves right through the hand or through the foot with their own rifles so they wouldn't have to go. They knew what was coming. Everybody knew what was coming, but didn't know which day.

Then, word came that we were to pack our things and get ready to board the planes. We were getting ready about 10:00 or 10:30 that evening on Sunday, June 3rd, 1944. We picked up everything we had and went to the airplanes in trucks. We had our M-1s and 150 rounds of ammunition. Each of us had a rope in case we got caught in a tree and had to climb down. We had candy bars and pills. They even gave us French money so we wouldn't steal from the French. We were told that if we took something, we should pay for it. We had rations of some kind. I remember the candy bars more than the rations.

When we got up to the planes, I remember that I had a dollar bill. Some of guys signed it. I left it with someone, although I don't remember who. I've still got it.

Sgt. Pipelow, the motor pool sergeant, said, "Fred, I'm going to help you get in that plane with the Colonel." That was because I used to take my car to the motor pool and get it fixed all the time. "You know, Fred, if you ever get back from this thing, you can always tell your kids that you were a little bitty cog in this big operation."

I didn't know where we were going to fly, so the Colonel told me. He said we were going to fly west toward the States and out over the ocean until we were all regrouped. Then, a submarine was going to come up with a red light. When that light was shown, the echelon of planes was to rendevous somewhere between England and Ireland. That's where all the planes would get together and turn to fly to Normandy. When we hit the coast of France we were to fly eight minutes and jump out. That should put us close to our objective.

I knew where Father Verret was going to be the first night. I think he was going to jump with Col. Maloney. I was in Col. Millet's plane and was supposed to jump with him. The jeep and the sergeant manning the jeep's machine gun were to be dropped somewhere near him, too.

Then all of a sudden we were told that we weren't going after all because of weather conditions. So we just stayed where we were and slept right on the ground out there. We had to wait all the next day, and didn't know when we were going again. I didn't see the Colonel at all the next day. We were just unorganized with everything. Everybody ate here or there that whole night and the next day. We didn't even know if we were going to go the next night. Then all of a sudden we were told to get into the planes.

* * * * *

3. D-Day

The next night, Monday, June 5th, 1944, was organized confusion getting into the planes. I never saw the Colonel, and he didn't see me because we weren't in the same plane. We took a long time to get organized with the different planes. We took off just before midnight, and flew out over the ocean and turned and went toward France. All of our planes were C-47s. The submarine with a red light came up and we flew over it, then we turned and we flew toward Normandy, France. We reached land about 2:00 a.m. Then we were supposed to head for Amfreville (west of the Merderet River, about 1,000 yards north of Amfreville) and rendevous. But it didn't happen that way at all. If we could have stayed up a few minutes longer we would have been in the right place. Men in some of the planes jumped out too soon. Some of them jumped right into the Channel and drowned. There was no way they were going to get out of the Channel. I don't remember when we crossed the Channel, but when we were getting closer to Normandy, I could see flack coming up.

As we got ready to go, it was about 2:30 a.m. I was the fourth one in my "stick" to jump out of the plane. We had to get up from both sides and interchange our jumps. The door was opened and we stood up. The Jump Master said, "Stand up and hook up." We were already standing up so that whenever the Jump Master said, "Go!" we would go.

I remember looking out the door at the plane next to us since I had one foot almost up to the door. I saw flack hit that plane. It burst into flames before it blew all to pieces. I asked myself, "What am I doing here?" I thought, "Oh, I hope I get out of here pretty quick." Just then the Jump Master said, "OK, we're going!" and we went.

They told us not to put any ammunition in our rifles until we hit the ground, but only fix our bayonets. If we came close to somebody, we should use the bayonet. We weren't to shoot anybody from a distance. If we did, we'd give away our position right away.

Preparing to jump on D-day.

I figure we jumped about two minutes too soon. I imagine some of the planes ended up in the right place, but they were so few that I don't think it made that much difference. We ended up wrong, but maybe it ended up better this way. Who knows? We've talked about it so much over the years at conventions. I just don't know. Some say, "Well, if I just had that other gun I wanted over there." But what if it got dropped in the water or they got dropped on the land. If it got dropped in the water, they'd never find it.

The French didn't know if they should be on our side or the Germans' side. They knew the Germans were friendly with them at that point, but that was only so the Germans could get all they could out of the French. Then when we came, no one knew if the French would be friendly to us or not.

* * * * *

I was at a convention in Colorado Springs, and saw a fellow I was with on the ground in Normandy for four days. He's the head of the 507th organization, and puts out our magazine. I asked him, "What happened after you hit the ground?"

He said, "I didn't even wait until I got out of the airplane before I made a booboo. I was in the front of the 'stick.' They told us to stand up and hook up. I was up by the door, about the third or fourth one who was going to go out."

After he stood up, he slipped and fell backwards. His rifle got caught on a piece of metal by the door, and he couldn't unhook it since it was underneath his chute. Somebody yelled, "Tell that guy to get the hell out of the way so we can get out the door." He tried to get out of the way, but somebody just pushed him and he went right out the door. They knew his chute would open, or figured it would. As he went out the door, his rifle broke right in two because it was right across the door.

When he got on the ground, at first there wasn't a

soul around. But in about 10 minutes he saw some Germans. He didn't shoot at them because he was all alone. He knew they'd just turn around and shoot him if he didn't get them first. Then one of them saw him and shot. He was hit in the leg and couldn't move. Somebody else saw him and shot at him from a different direction. He couldn't walk or do anything. He just laid there until they came to get him and take him prisoner. They took him to a truck and drove him from one place to another. Finally, they got him to a German hospital with a doctor and he was taken care of. He was prisoner in a hospital someplace in France. It was eventually overrun by the Americans, and he was liberated. He went back to England and then home. He was only on the ground 10 minutes before the Germans had him.

* * * * *

My landing was the nicest, softest one of any jump I'd made. The air was so heavy that it made for a real nice landing. That was my twelfth jump. I had a beautiful landing right in the middle of some trees. I was all alone. No matter where you are, even if you're in the middle of the Nebraska Sand Hills, you'd see somebody. But here I didn't see anybody.

The Germans were on higher ground. They had flooded a lot of the land just before D-Day. They stuck sharp-pointed sticks into the ground pointing up into the air. If you landed on one of those sticks, you could get hurt. Whole fields were full of them in different places. That was that German general's idea. He came in and did those things. It really caused a lot of problems for us.

When I got on the ground, I remember looking at my watch. It was 2:40 in the morning on Tuesday, June 6th. They wanted everybody to have a watch so I bought an Army watch. The Germans took it from me later. I didn't see anybody, but I heard something. I rolled up my chute like I was told and put it by a tree. Then I started to walk a little bit. The password for us on D-day was "Thunder" instead of "Halt, who goes there." We answered with "Welcome." I was glad we had that rather than the cricket sound like the 101st used. They were supposed to repeat it with another cricket. But the Germans figured that out on the first or

Paratroopers Jumping from an Airplane.
(Source: *A Wartime Log*)

second day. They learned to make the same sound by clicking their rifles. The cricket sound was just like hitting a rifle bolt quickly. The Germans hit their rifle bolts quick and it sounded almost like the cricket sound. So I was glad that we had what we did.

I walked around for a while. I didn't see anyone at all on the ground because the trees and hedgerows were so thick. It was 6:30 in the morning before I saw anyone – seven Germans. I knew there were seven because I could count them, and I knew they were Germans because they didn't look like we did. I heard them talking so I just ducked down. I didn't do anything but wait and see if I could find some other GIs. That was the best thing to do. Later I ran into a couple of Americans and then a couple more. I didn't know which Company they belonged to, but it seemed I ended up with GIs from 3rd Battalion. I had no idea where the Colonel was or where the jeep had been dropped. A jeep had been dropped later on D-day, and I saw it go by – the Germans had it. They were shooting the machine gun back at us.

We were supposed to rendevous with the Regiment at a corner just outside of Amfreville about 1:30 or 2:00 in the afternoon on D-Day. But we never did get together because we landed right in the German 91st Division. They had just moved into that area. That changed a lot of things and we had no idea where we were.

Our objective was to knock out the bridges around the town of Amfreville. We tried to cut down anything we could – electricity or communication. If we saw a wire, we cut it. Somebody always had something to cut with. The objective was to disrupt their communication, bridges, and highways to keep stuff from moving on.

* * * * *

The days ran into nights and the night were just like days. You just go, go, go. You draw arm fire and they shoot, and you just shoot back if you see somebody. You could be shooting at your own men because you really didn't know who was there. It was like that on Tuesday and Tuesday night (June 6th). It was the same all day Wednesday, all night Wednesday, and Thursday. We'd get a few Germans as prisoners, then they'd crawl off at night and they got some of us as prisoners and some of us would crawl off. We were right in with the Germans all the time. We never really knew who was just right next to us. We were that close. We were trying to get to the Blue Task Force. There were Blue and Red Task Forces.

On Thursday (June 8th), we ran and ran and ran. We could barely breathe or barely move. Still, we had big hedge rows or vines to climb over that were as high as a wall. Normally we could have crawled over them, but we were so damn tired that we couldn't. Sometimes we just ran right over graves that were only two feet deep. They were big, open spots back in the woods, 10 feet by 20 feet. The Germans dug them anyway they could and just put the GIs in them. I think they took the Germans somewhere else. I ran right over the top of those graves and just kept running with whoever was with me. I was so uptight from running across some of these graves. I didn't even know if all the people in them were dead or not. We just kept going. I never got hungry until the second day after I was taken prisoner. Then I realized I was exhausted.

We just got to where we couldn't handle it any more. We just more or less petered out. That's the way I felt that fourth day, Thursday. I was exhausted and never even knew where the front line was. We were with the Germans and they were with us. We were organized confusion, and they were, too. We knew where they were almost better than they knew where we were. That's the way it was.

I was with about 100 to 150 men most of the time on Wednesday, Thursday, Friday, and Friday night. We'd be with somebody during the night or during the day, and we kind of knew who we were with – so and so or so and so. I didn't know the enlisted men in the 3rd Battalion. I knew the officers better than the enlisted men because I was around them more than the enlisted men. Then the next day, we'd be with somebody else. I never did see anyone from the 101st Airborne, but we weren't really supposed to either. There were people from the 82nd I knew, but I didn't know them very well. I was with a couple of guys I knew for a while. Even though I knew them by their first names, I didn't see them the next day. Then I ran into two more guys I didn't know. I didn't even know where they came from. I didn't know if they were 508th, 507th, or some other outfit.

On the fourth and fifth days (Thursday and Friday), I was so uptight that I didn't know if I wanted to go on any further. "Why don't I just stop and let them take me or hit me? Then I'd be done." That's how it was each day. It was another day. We thought, "If I can just stay alive..." We'd say to each other, "I'm glad I'm here right now. I don't know where I'll be in half an hour."

Guys got hurt or killed and you couldn't do anything. There was nothing we could do. If someone got hurt, the others would just go and leave them there. That's the way it was for all those days. There was always someone getting killed at night when we were walking. The guy behind me got killed, then the guy behind him got killed. When someone got hurt, all we could do was make him comfortable and keep going. We didn't stay with anybody, even if he was a good friend of ours, and he wouldn't stay with us either. What could you do if the guy who was the commanding officer said, "Come on. Let's go."?

* * * *

Then it was Friday, June 9th. We had been there Tuesday, Wednesday, Thursday, and Friday. It was day and night, just one after the other. And we had all been together. It got so that I couldn't even eat a candy bar. I wasn't even hungry. I didn't even think of water or things like that.

On Friday afternoon, I was with a group of about 25 men walking across an open field when we heard some trucks and half tracks. I'm not sure if it was the same group I'd been with a half day or even an hour before. We got into a hedgerow right along side of a road. In the road were German tanks, trucks, and machinery of all kinds going in the direction of the beach.

We were hiding in there and there was nothing we could do. I looked out into the field and saw about a half dozen cows. A French lady came wearing a long dress. She had three kids. One kid was quite small, about two years old. They each had a milk bucket. The lady carried a milk bucket and a stool. She sat down by a cow and milked it right out there while the half tracks drove by and we were in the hedgerow.

As we were in the hedgerow we tried to find out who was the commanding officer. We found out it was a Captain Taylor by asking down the row, "Who's the commanding officer here?"

We passed along, "I think its Captain Taylor, 3rd Battalion. He's in this end up here."

Someone said, "If you talk, talk low. If you smoke, fan the smoke." Then we counted off in both directions. There were 28 of us. I was number 14 in the middle, so I figure there were about 28.

Captain Taylor said, "We're going to stay here now. It's about 4:30 in the afternoon. We'll stay here until it gets dark, then we'll move out. After we walk between a half mile and a mile, we should hit some flooded water. You might have to put your weapon over your head and carry it that way. Don't worry about the rest of yourself. You might have to go into the water up to your head." That's what each person passed along to whomever was next to him. That was the only time I really felt like I could sit down and not run, run, run all the time.

We stayed there until it was 11:00 p.m. It was pitch dark. The vehicles were off the road quite a long time, so Captain Taylor moved us out. He said, "If you draw fire, hit the ground. That's all you can do. Then get up and just keep going. If you shoot at anybody, make sure you can see them and know who it is. You could be shooting at one of our own men."

We walked for probably an hour. We drew fire once in a while and we'd hit the ground. Somebody would say that all was clear and we'd get up. Then somebody drew fire again. They could see us moving, but we didn't know who they were or where they were. We kept moving.

I noticed an opening. I didn't think of it at the time, but it was a big opening in the field where wagons and horses drove into a field to work. We walked through that field. It wasn't long before we saw the barrel of two big 88 mm guns sticking out. They couldn't hit us because we were right under them. We walked further following Captain Taylor. He knew exactly where we were trying to go, but we were right under the 88s. They were all pointed in one direction – toward the Channel. They were manned and I could hear the Germans talking and clanking their canteens, belts, guns, shells, or something. They were talking to one another as if something was coming.

* * * *

4. Captured!

All of a sudden flares went up and it was as light as day. We were walking in a column about 40 or 50 feet long in the field. The first four men were out across the field, which wasn't real big – just enough for those two 88s. There was another gate that about four of the men went through, and the Germans shot them. I don't know what happened to those four. They may have been killed or wounded. Everybody else fell to the ground when the flares went off.

The German soldiers surrounded us and told us to drop our rifles on the ground. I don't remember if any of them spoke in English or not, but we all had hit the ground. The first thing I knew, they were feeling where my wrist watch was. They took my watch right away. They went through our pockets and got what they wanted. Then they made us get up and stand there as they got us all together. Then the flares had died down and it got darker. It was 3:00 a.m., Saturday, June 10th.

The German soldiers made us walk. We hadn't walked very far, maybe a quarter of a mile, when we came to a barn and farm house. A German general had just moved into that area and was in the house. Guards were around the house and the farm. We went into the farm yard and they pointed to the barn. We went in.

When I got into the barn, I saw a guy who was moaning and hurt. He had been hit in the groin by a wooden bullet. His wound had burst open and was gangrene because he had been sitting there for a day or two. The Germans had been shooting at us with wooden bullets. They had been there on maneuvers and weren't going to use their metal bullets. The wooden ones were actually worse at close range. Sometimes they were so close to us that when they shot somebody, the wood stayed in the person's body. If the bullet had gone all the way through, it would have been better.

Someone asked, "Would you go get some water?"

I said, "I'll go get it."

I knew I had seen a pump when I came in. One the Germans had been leaning on it. There was a little board platform around the pump to stand on to pump water. I stood up there and was going to use my helmet to pump water into. I looked down and saw a helmet on the ground. I reached for it, and I saw a "chicken" on it. I knew that helmet. It was the Colonel's. He must have been taken earlier on the same day and in the same area that we were. I filled his helmet with water and took it into the barn. I said to somebody, "This is the Colonel's helmet." We stayed there that night.

The next day the Germans lined us up and made us start walking. We walked to a place where there were some trucks. At first they didn't know if they were going to let us get in the trucks or not. Then they decided they weren't going to let us in. They said, "Just walk." because they wanted to ride in the truck. Why put us in the truck? So we walked several miles that day.

We walked for a couple of days. I didn't know if we were going toward Alençon or Paris. As we walked, there were always planes flying over that came down and strafed us. We had to get out of the way and duck down. Once we got out on the highway, we know they were taking us to Alençon.

When we got to Alençon, they put us inside of a fence for prisoners – Americans, French, or whomever they wanted to put there. We were mostly all Americans because there were no British in that area. At least, I didn't see any. I had been in there only a short time and it was getting toward evening. Then I saw the Colonel. He was talking to a German guard or officer.

He and I started to talk when all of a sudden they took him. They took him away fast. They said, "Come!" or "Aus mit din!," so he went with them. That was the last time I ever saw him. I knew then that he had been taken prisoner. (The Colonel got back home after the war, and he wrote to me once. His wife divorced him. And as far as I know, it was not too long after that he died. I never did see him again.)

The next day we started to walk again. We walked quite a while. This included five nights and two rainy days, and we didn't get any food from the "Jerries." We saw trenches and ditches about three or four feet deep along the road that had been dug by the French and Italians. They were on both sides of the road almost all the way to Paris. They were just low enough to get in and duck down when airplanes flew over us. By now, we were riding in the trucks. If a plane came, the truck stopped. The drivers saw the planes coming and got out first. They made us stay in the truck while they got into the trenches. They pointed their guns at us to make us stay there. We waved white flags or anything that would show, but the airplanes still shot at us. We found that out real quick, because they'd just pepper us. If we got out of the truck and crawled under it, that wasn't so bad. We found out the Germans would let us do that. We were strafed quite often along the way.

We got to Falasie, better known to us as Notre Dame or Starvation Hill on Tuesday, June 20th. We stayed there until Friday night, June 23rd. We were left in the truck, but after a while they made us get out and walk.

When we got close to Alençon on Monday, June 26th, we stopped at what I figured was a Catholic girls school, which was on top of a hill. It had been turned into a camp with a fence all around it. All of the books had been taken outside. There was a beautiful organ in the school, but all of the books and anything else of any value were gone. There was nothing in the church except straw on the floor. We stayed in the church.

One of the prisoners I was with was an officer and a P-47 fighter pilot. He came in and saw that organ. He could play anything on that organ, just like Liberace. He bounced that organ around like you wouldn't believe with those 1939 and 1940 songs. The Germans were up there just as fast as you please and told him to get off that organ and get out of there. They didn't want anyone feeling that good. That guy could play the organ!

They asked if somebody would go for water, and I said I'd go. I was always trying to see what was going on without volunteering for something I shouldn't do. We walked down a steep hill, got hot water, and took it back up the hill. That's what we drank. The Germans started to give us hot water right away so we wouldn't get diarrhea. We were there a day and two nights. Then they took us to Chartres by truck on Sunday, July 9th.

* * * * *

We had horses in the column between Alençon and Chartres. The horses got shot during an airplane strafing, and one horse died. The Germans started to butcher it, and asked if I'd help. I took the knife, and they said, "Go ahead." So I helped them butcher the horse. There was a big iron pot about four feet across and three feet deep in a church yard near Chartres. They put a wood cover over the pot, and built a big fire under it in the church yard. They put the horse meat in – bones and all – and cooked it. We ate horse soup that day.

The German who told me to help them pulled out a big bone with lots of meat on it for me. That was the first time I relaxed. I never relaxed before with all that running, shooting, and fighting. I was uptight like you wouldn't believe. So was everyone else. We ate the horse meat and then started out again.

* * * * *

We stayed in Chartres from July 9th until 4:00 p.m on

Saturday, July 15th. We arrived in Paris later that same day. When we got to Paris, they packed 36 of us into a train box car. They opened two doors pushed us all in, and later pushed us all out. There weren't any steps or gates or anything. It was so tight that we couldn't sit down because their box cars are shorter than ours. If one person knelt down, the other ones couldn't. Somebody had to stand all the time. We couldn't see out because there were no windows.

We were in the Paris marshaling yards near the railroad yard for four or five days. We stayed there and they never let us out for six days and nights. If we had to piss, we just did it through the cracks in the box cars. I wondered why the hell they left us sitting there.

We got out of the train in Paris and got into a truck. I remember being in a covered truck and looking out the back end. I saw the Eiffel Tower and people on the street in Paris. They were not very friendly. I thought they would be friendlier. Maybe they weren't sure whose side they should take. They may have thought that the German are treating them pretty good and we were the guys causing all the ruckus. If people on the street went into the bathrooms, we could see their legs or see them sit down on the seat. It struck me to see it right out in the open.

We were in trucks for quite a ways until we got to the outskirts of Paris. Paris was declared an open city, which meant that neither the Americans nor the Germans were supposed to bomb it. They didn't want to ruin Paris, even though they hit and wrecked Cologne and other cities. They bombed the shit out of them in Germany, but they did agree not to bomb Paris.

Since Paris was an open city, we knew we were safe from strafing and bombing. Planes went over but they didn't drop any bombs. If a plane didn't know where it was and dropped a bomb, it was only by accident. They really kept that city open. I wondered if other cities were open, but they mustn't have been. The closer we got to Germany, the more the cities had been bombed.

* * * * *

After we left Paris, we went by train to Château-Thierry, Sézanne, Nancy, and then north to Metz, France. They took us underneath the railroad station in Metz because the Allies had bombed the place like you wouldn't believe. We went down some steps, crossed over, and went down more steps. They must have built those steps years before. They took us to an air raid shelter under the train station. We were down there a couple of days.

During the first night, I woke up about 1:00 a.m. because I had already taken a nap. I saw two German guards sitting at a rough, old table drinking beer. I walked over to see what time it was and made it known that I would like some beer even though I didn't speak any German. One of them said, "Ja."and pushed a beer over to me. I sat down with him and drank it. Later on when we were in Frankfurt, he gave me another beer.

We left Metz and went up the Mossell River through Trier and Koblenz. From there we went up the Rhine River to Frankfurt am Main, Germany.

One of our German guards broke his rifle as we went up the Rhine River. We got strafed several times going up there. During one air raid alarm, we jumped quickly out of the train box cars and ran toward a cave on the bank of the river. The box car door opening was quite small. The German guard had his rifle strapped over his shoulder rather than pointed straight ahead. The rifle was sideways as he jumped out of the train car and it broke right in two. The German guards and we prisoners all laughed that it happened.

The land is wide open, just like it is in South Dakota or North Dakota. Tanks could run right across it in a couple of hours because it was that kind of country. We were out there with nothing else around us. Then the Allied fighters came. I don't know why they didn't hit the length of the train. Instead, they came through the side of the train. They hit part of the train with tracer bullets setting it on fire. Then they went around for another pass. They came around again and fired and set another car on fire. That disrupted the whole train, but it didn't hurt all of it. I still don't know if they were trying to save the trains or not.

After the Allied planes left, we all got outside and pushed the cars apart. Everyone did this – prisoners, guards, and all. If we laid down or sat down, they pointed their guns at us and we got up. We pushed the damaged cars to the side of the tracks, got back in the cars, and eventually got going again. By this time, we were getting close to Frankfurt.

Sometimes I thought, "Here I am a prisoner. I never dreamed I'd be taken prisoner." Then the next minute, I'd think, "I'm kind of relieved." The next day I'd think, "Well, I'm still here. Why am I still here and those guys back there are gone? I could have been one of them." Then the next day, I'd think, "I'm still here." Then we'd go on. We'd get strafed and someone would get killed by the Germans, and I'd say, "I'm still here." Then we'd go further and the whole train got bombed. Some of the men got wounded and some were gone, and I'd think, "I'm still here in this train."

The Germans were very good at camouflage, in fact, they were excellent. They were as good as anybody – better than the Americans. It took a long time to get from Paris to Frankfurt because we were in this open area. At one point, we were on the ground and I saw a big open spot with trees around it. It looked like a hill or mound in the field. We stopped and picked up rocks at these places so they could build an air strip for their fighters. They wanted an air strip right here and used us to pick up the rocks. We didn't have to pick up the rocks, but they could shoot us. So we did what we were told.

They had some places made already. They dug caves in hills. Whole hills were caves with tops made of wood or steel. I couldn't believe what I was watching. They had the hills covered with trees and stumps set in pots. They used a bunch of little tractors and pulled all the trees out of the field so they couldn't be seen from the air. When their fighters came, they talked to them below and told them not to land, but to fly around one more time and come in later when the American planes left. Then they would roll the trees back so their planes could land and go into the caves. There were places like that all the way back through Germany. The landing strip couldn't be seen from the air, and no one would know those planes were right there under the ground with trees over the top of the thing.

We stood there and watched the whole thing. Once in a while there were dog fights going on. We just laid in the sun and watched the dog fights. If an American was shot down and was coming down in his parachute, we tried to get as close to him as possible to get information. We were always looking for how thing were going. He may have been shot down, but at least he knew how the war was doing. Once a pilot was captured, he was right there with us, just one of us. They separated us later, but just then we were with everybody – Americans, British, officers, enlisted.

* * * * *

When we got outside of Frankfurt, there were big barracks, like an army base. They let us out of the trucks and we went in. They put us in solitary rooms. There was nothing in my room except a cot and a couple of blankets – one for the bottom, one for the top. I didn't really need the top blanket because it was July and it wasn't very cold in those cells. They made me take off all of my clothes and took them away except for my coveralls. Everything I had was taken except my rosary. When I walked and didn't have a rosary, I used my fingers just like a rosary. There was a shutter on the window so I couldn't see anyone, but everyday at different hours, I could hear the American bombers going over. At night, I could hear the British going over.

In the morning they brought me a glass or bottle with water in it. I think the water was heated when I first got it because the longer I kept it, the cooler it got. When I had to go to the bathroom, I just went in the pail that they gave me. I hardly ever had to go to the bathroom because I never had much to eat. I was there for two solid weeks and never knew why. Once I heard other guys making noises by stomping their feet, pounding on the wall, or hollering out loud. I stayed within myself and didn't do anything like that. Every noon they brought the same thing – two slices of bread with blackish molasses in between.

One day a German guard came. I could hear the sound of his boots as he came toward the door. He opened the door and said, "Heraus! Come with me." All I was wearing was my coveralls. I went with him down the hallway, down another, then down another one. We went into a small, nice-looking office. There sat a nice looking, blond-haired German fellow. He spoke very good English – better than I spoke.

He said, "Hello, Fred. You're going to be a part of the German Reich for as long as you live. We're going to take you to a camp where you can plant a garden, grow vegetables, and help us with the work around the camp. You're going to be with us forever – all your life. You'll have a good home."

He talked a little more and offered me a cigarette. I said I didn't smoke. He had Camels, Lucky, and Chesterfields on the desk that I'm sure came from the States, maybe from Red Cross boxes. He asked me if I wanted a beer. I took a beer and drank it warm.

We visited for a while, and he said, "I don't have to ask you any questions. I know all about your outfit. I know where you were. I know everything about when you were over in the United States. I know you came over on the Stratenaver, and when you were in Ireland."

Then he said, "Here's a Red Cross box." He gave me the box, and I left. Later on I looked in the box and thought, "Oh boy. This is the only thing I've got to my name – just that box and my life."

One of the things in the Red Cross box was toothpaste. I really appreciated that. I never had my teeth fixed until I got home. When I got home, I knew that the Army would send me on furlough, and I wanted to be sure to get my teeth looked at. But when I was a prisoner, I thought my teeth were going to fall out, even though I still had them all. I always wondered why my teeth hadn't fallen out since I had been a prisoner so long.

From talking to that German officer, it seemed that he and I could have been friends. He was so easy to talk to. It felt like he wanted to be nice to me, and I don't know why. I didn't try to make a big issue out of being all alone in solitary. He knew all that. He knew a whole lot more about me than I knew about him. I think he did me a favor by sending me to the camp where I ended up. He could have sent me to any one of the other camps.

After I returned to the U.S., I talked to a minister in Yankton. He told me that they could have sent me to Poland or Czechoslovakia. He said that he was a prisoner on a farm and had hardly anything to eat. He had to work every single day. I was a T-Sergeant and that helped me when I went to my camp. (All the G.I.s at Stalag Luft IV were sergeants.) I heard there was another paratrooper in the camp but in another compound. I didn't know anyone else there. I only saw that German officer that one day. I still think he sent me to the camp on purpose. I was just lucky that I got to that camp because of the way I ended up. I got home anyway.

* * * * *

A German guard asked me, "How come your name is Peschl? Where are you from?" I told him that Peschl is an Austrian name. Before coming to America, my dad lived closer to Austria than to Germany. There are many Peschls in Austria, but they spell their names a little differently. Some are Poschl and some are Peschel. When my dad came over to America, he was at the courthouse in Yankton and had to decide what his name was going to be. They said to him, "Make your name as short as you can." So he dropped the "e" between the "h" and the "l."

* * * * *

We left Frankfurt am Main in late July and went north by train to Wetzlar. We went through Narburg, Kassel, and Magdeburg. We arrived in Berlin during the night and left again the next morning. From there we went to Stetten and Gross-Tychow in Pomerania. This was to be our new home, if you can call it that. We arrived at Stalag Luft IV, which is in the middle of a heavily wooded pine area at 7:00 a.m. on Friday, August 4th. I didn't realize we were so close to the Baltic Sea, but it was cold up there in fall and winter.

* * * * *

The first time Marcie heard that I was missing was when Father Verret wrote a letter to her. He told her that I was missing but didn't know where I was. He knew Marcie because she had been with me all the time when I was in training. Father Verret started with our unit in the States and stayed with us the whole time. He was our original Padre. I knew him from the first day I jumped. He jumped, too. I don't know when he jumped during Parachute School, but he was in the company when they were first activated back in Georgia. He was with us in Alliance, Nebraska. He jumped with us in Denver and, of course, on D-day.

Father Verret wrote a letter to Marcie, which said:

"I received your letter yesterday asking about Fred. I don't know where the Alliance people got its information, but I'm quite sure it was not from me. However, there is some truth in it. Freddie is missing, Mrs. Peschl, and to the best of my knowledge, he is a prisoner. He was in good health when last seen about June 16th. He was captured about the 9th or 10th, I believe. Outside of that, I can't say. As soon as anything is established, you will be notified. Fred was a good friend of mine, Mrs. Peschl, and you know how dearly he loved you and his little son. His pinups consisted entirely of your pictures. He is a good lad, was faithful to Mass and the Sacraments. I am sure God will protect him for you. I owe a lot to Fred for the many little favors he did for me. And if there is any way I can repay by helping you, please don't hesitate to ask. God bless you and the baby. Capt. Verret."

Father Verret got killed in the Battle of the Bulge. He was taking some wounded to the Red Cross wagon. They shouldn't ever make a direct hit on a Red Cross truck, but that's exactly what the Germans did. He was the only one who was killed while they were doing this. The others were helping, but he was killed with a direct hit of an 88. That's a big gun. He was sure a nice person.

Joe Poplawski also wrote to Marcie. His letter said:

"Dear Marcie, I received your letter and was very surprised to hear from you. Well Marcie, I'm sorry to say, but I, too, don't know anything about Freddie and it seems that the First Sergeant doesn't know anything about him. You see, the last time I saw Freddie was the Thursday following D-Day. He was with the Colonel then when I saw him, but about that time we all sort of had to separate. Please Marcie, let me know in case you find out anything.

And how is Terry making out. I guess he's quite the boy now. Hoping everything is alright. Hope this gets to you and you'll find out everything about Freddie."

They let me write a card to Marcie from Frankfurt am Main, a little over a month after I was captured (July 24, 1944). I wrote:

"Dearest Marcie and Terry boy, I am a prisoner of war in Germany and just fine and getting along OK. Not hurt in any way. Don't write to this address. Will forward new address later. Happy anniversary and birthday. All my love to you both, mama and dad. Your loving husband, Fred."

* * * * *

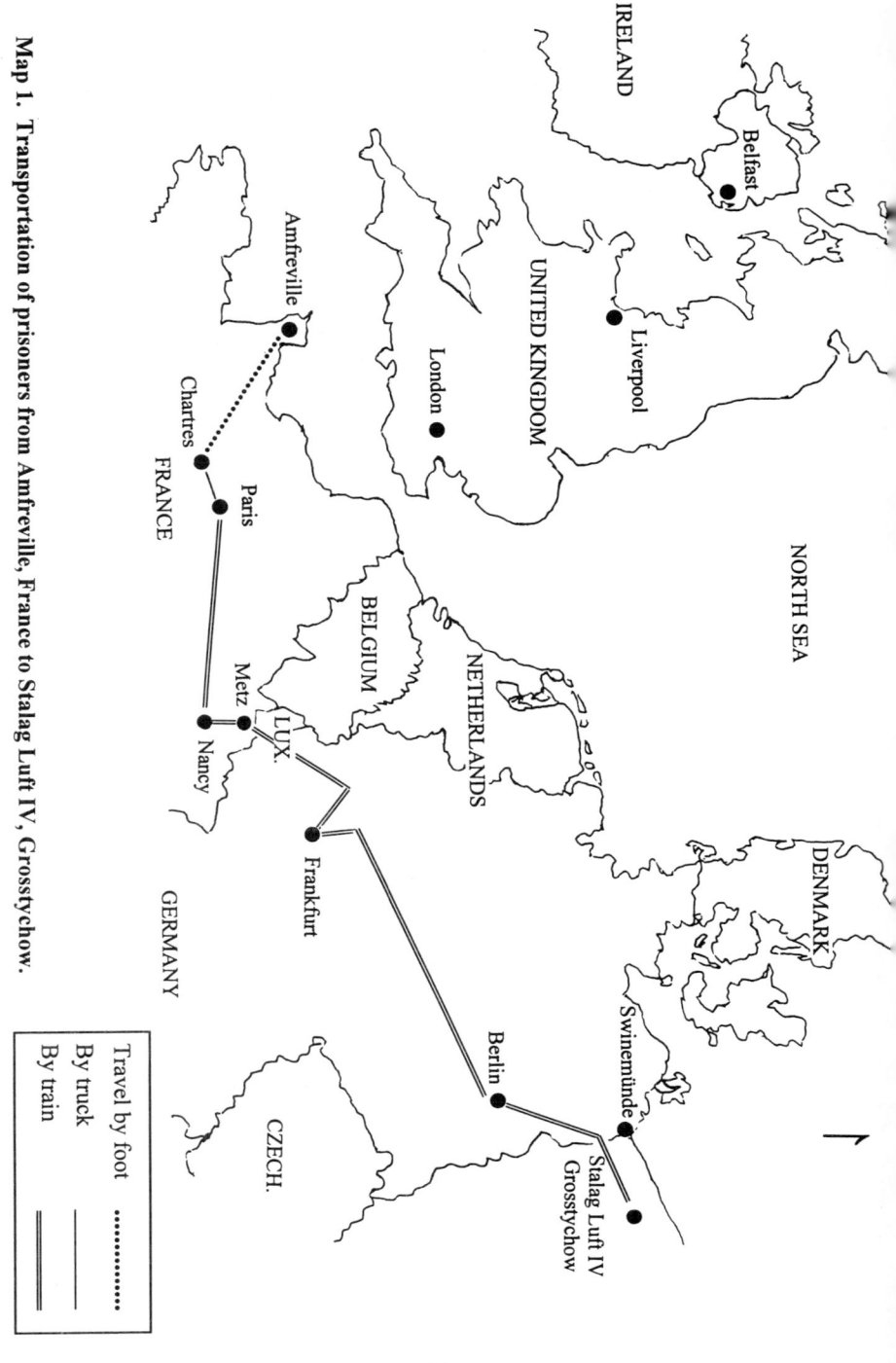

Map 1. Transportation of prisoners from Amfreville, France to Stalag Luft IV, Grosstychow.

5. Stalag Luft IV

We arrived at the Kiefheide railroad station. It was the train stop for Stalag Luft IV near Grosstychow (in what is now Poland) and the Baltic Sea, and got out of the box car. We were met by a red-headed German captain in a white uniform with a big iron cross and other medals. Each of us was given a Red Cross box to carry. Then the German captain and the guards got us into a group and started us toward the prison camp a couple miles away. At first, we walked or marched about 100 yards at a normal pace. But then they used their guns and bayonets to make us walk faster and faster and faster. Then we went double time until we were running. They jabbed us with the bayonets and gun butts to make us run faster, especially those on the outside of the group. If anyone slowed down, they were hit with the butt of a rifle or jabbed with a bayonet. The German captain shouted to make the guards force us to move faster. The guards shouted at us and guard dogs nipped at our legs the whole way. They were just cruel. I got several bad bites on my legs.

Some of the prisoners dropped their coats, Red Cross packages, and anything else they were carrying. When the guys dropped their Red Cross boxes and other things they were carrying, they weren't jabbed any more. The guards wanted our boxes and that's why they jabbed us. They couldn't just take them away from us, but they could jab us so we'd drop them as we ran. I dropped mine, but I still had those dog bites on my legs.

When we arrived at the camp we were herded into the Vorlager. Then they started to be nicer to us. I still don't know why they changed their attitude so quickly. I heard later that the German captain's wife and children had been killed by the Allied bombing, and he was trying to get even with us.

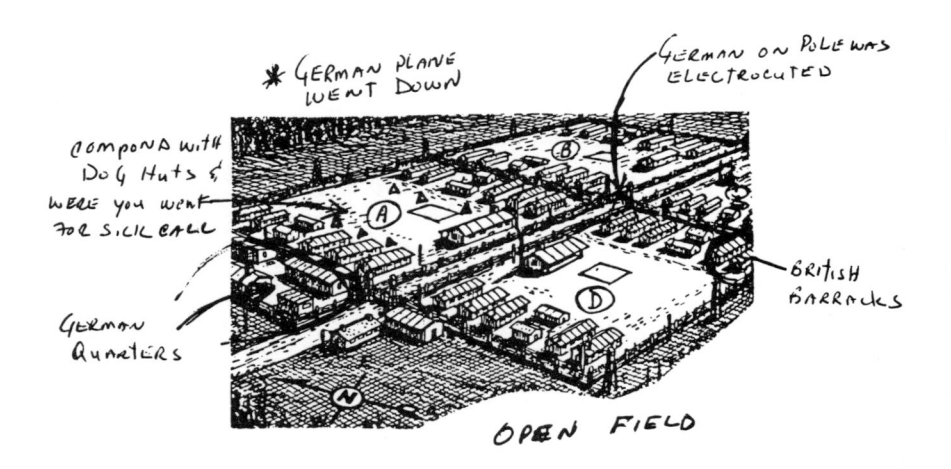

* * * * *

Line drawing of Stalag Luft IV.
(Source: letter from Leonard E. Rose)

The guards gave us instructions about what they wanted us to know in the same part of the camp where we got our shots. We were there all day as they gave us instructions. After those initial instructions, they gave a few more instructions to us *Kriegies* (the German word for "war prisoners") almost everyday. They would always tell us something different – "You'd better do this." or "You'd better not do that." Mostly it was, "Don't touch that warning wire." It wasn't just not touching the wire, it was best not even to get close to it. There were two barbed wire fences 10 feet high around the camp. I heard the outside fence was electrical. The warning wire was 50 feet from the first 10-foot barbed wire fence.

* * * * *

There was an English doctor at the camp, Capt. Pollock who was in another compound. I asked him what I should do about my leg because it was full of the dog bites I got when I first arrived at the camp.

He said, "You got a tetanus shot when you came into the camp. But everyday that you can, lay in the sun as long as possible. Have the place where the dogs bit you facing the sun. It's August, and it's warm. That will do you more good that anything I can give you. I can't even give you a pill because I haven't even got an aspirin. Do that at least."

And I did. I took my pants off some of the time or rolled up my pant leg and laid in the sun. The bites got better after a while.

* * * * *

I met Howard Fahr and Art Schwegert at the camp. We were all in the same room — Lager A, Barracks A, Room 5. We tried to keep as active as we could in the barracks. Everyday we got up and went out for a walk around the whole compound. I walked around there many, many times during the nice, warm days of summer. I'd always go out and visit somebody or go someplace else in our compound if I could.

We could never get more than seven fellows together in any one group. If there were more than seven of us standing and visiting, say if there were nine people, the guards could shoot into the group with machine guns. They could do that legally, and they told us that ahead of time.

We had to be back in the compound by 4:00. We were counted at 4:30, so we didn't go very far. The farthest we could go was about 50 yards away from your barracks. If we walked all the way around the compound, we would have walked about the length of a city block. I walked around it many times. I always picked up a buddy and visited about something back home. I knew a guy from Brooklyn who would say, "If I was home I could hera the boyds choypin'." That's how they talked in Brooklyn and New York. "You could hera the boyds choypin'."

Hand drawing of POWs' room at Stalag Luft IV by Howard Farr.

(Source: *A Wartime Log*)

* * * * *

In early November, 1944, a few months after I arrived in the camp, the Red Cross sent copies of a book called *A Wartime Log*. It was a white, cloth-covered book with empty pages where we could write down the things that were happening to us.

There were supposed to be enough books so that each one of the 20 men in our room could have one, but there was only enough for two books per room. We drew cards to see who would win them. I was lucky enough to draw the 9 of Clubs and get one of the books. I wrote a few lines in it nearly every day.

Nov 4, 44 — "Nov 4th will be a date not to be forgotten very soon. Received my first letter from Marcie and Terry tonight and was happy to hear from them, and to know they are getting along OK."

Nov 5, 44 — "Today is the second Sunday that I have missed Mass, since I have been here. It's because we have been in quarantine for the past two weeks. Made myself some fried spuds and spam today. It was delicious."

Nov 6 — "Was real ambitious today and did some laundry, overalls, jacket, long johns, and etc. Also felt a little more homesick today that I usually do. Thought of Marcy and Terry all day."

I also took the book to other guys in the barracks and the compound and had them write things or draw in it. I'd go out and visit different people to try to find pencils. I always took everything back that I borrowed. I made sure I returned the pencils so that I could borrow them again.

Sunday Nov 19, 44 — "The choir sure sang nice at Mass this morning. It really makes me homesick when I hear the choir sing. Gordon Fisher drew the swell picture of Marcie in my Log today. Hope I get a picture of Terry soon so he can put it in."

* * * * *

Hand drawing of Marcy Peschl by Gordon Fisher.
(Source: *A Wartime Log*)

There was a tent outside in the yard of the camp. We took the poles out of the tent and used them for a baseball bat. We took old clothing and tied it up as tight as we could to make a soft ball. If we hit the ball, we'd barely make it to first base. We'd try to play ball or go for a walk.

Some of the Englishmen had been at the camp for a

long time, maybe since Dunkirk. They were there a long time. They could catch birds by their feet with a little string with a noose tied in it. They put it on the ground and gave it a tug when the bird stepped into the noose. They cleaned and ate the birds. I just heard about that, but I don't know how true it was. I know that some guys tried to catch little birds. I know what sparrows, black birds, and robins look like, but I don't know what those birds were over there. Every once in a while I saw a bird, but not very often. They'd say you could catch birds if you had lots of time and patience.

The prisoners argued a lot when they played cards. It wasn't that they argued so much about the cards themselves, but about airplanes. If one of the men was in a B-17, he'd argue that it was better than being in a B-24. The B-24 guys would argue that their plane was better. I always wanted to know that if they were all so good, why did they get shot down. They'd say, "Well, the Germans just happened to hit us."

We played a lot of whist card games. All the cards were made by the prisoners. They made whole decks of them by scrounging up boxes. The cards were homemade out of Red Cross boxes and marked with a red or pencil. They didn't have to play with a set of cards very long before they memorized what the card was by the markings on the back side.

There was some musical equipment in the camp. They also had some women's dresses. Some of the guys dressed up like women and put on plays. They were damn good. About every two or three weeks, we could go to the Red Cross room at 3:00 in the afternoon. We'd have a little show where somebody pulled out a guitar and sang. They didn't have a squeeze box, but there was a mouth organ and things like that. There was always someone there to play it. That's how we passed our time away.

The Kriege Katz were a small orchestra of the more talented men of the compound. They put on a little one-hour show for the benefit of the fellows in the compound. It was usually quite a good show.

The camp had a phonograph that was rotated from barracks to barracks. From time to time it was our turn to get the phonograph. We listened to Bing Crosby and the Mills Brothers.

It was tough when we couldn't get a hold of a book to read. There was nothing to read other than the prayer book.

* * * * *

They brought the Red Cross packages in by horse and an old lumber wagon. The same wagon was used to bring our clothes into the camp. The Red Cross boxes came from

Hand drawing that shows the delivery of Red Cross packages.
(Source: *A Wartime Log*)

America, Britain, or Canada. I'd always say, "Oh, I hope we get a Red Cross parcel this week." We liked the Canadian ones best. They had one lb. corned beef and one lb. spam, sardines in oil, half lb. salmon, twelve oz. white crackers, seven oz. raisins, six oz. prunes, one lb. cheese, half lb. sugar, coffee and tea, a qt. can of klim (powdered milk), a chocolate bar, salt and pepper, a lb. butter, and a 12 oz. can jam. The British and the American ones were real good, too. They had many of the same kinds of items in them. The American and British packages each had a bar of soap and of course everyone liked the American packages because there were cigarettes in them.

The Red Cross packages were an important part of our meals. We had a pitcher of hot water or Jerry coffee for breakfast at 7:30. The noon meal at 11:30 was potato soup, horse soup, bean soup, or plain soup. The evening meal at 4:30 was cooked spuds. Side dishes for the week included a loaf of dark bread, a half pound of butter, two ounces of cheese, and two ounces of jam.

I had a little box on the side wall. It was an empty Red Cross box about 1.5 feet long by 1.5 feet wide by 6 inches deep. There was a little piece of cigarette I was saving in that box. I'd put it there to use the next day.

If I had half a cigarette, a kid would say, "My dad's got a lot of money at home. I'll give you a hundred bucks when we get home if you'll give me that cigarette today."

I told him, "Well, that cigarette is worth something today, but what will it be worth when you get home?" I didn't care if somebody's dad was a millionaire at home. So it didn't really mean much.

* * * * *

When doors are locked
    And Goones a bed
    The cans are greased

And the stove is red
To cook the food that's hid away
That we may live another day.
So go to it, boys,
Cook, bake, and eat like kings.
For no one knows what tomorrow brings.

(Source: *A Wartime Log*)

* * * * *

The Germans went through everybody's mail. We couldn't write anything without them reading it all first. They read anything they wanted to read. If you wrote anything bad about them and sent it, they tore it up right away. So you just wrote things like, "Hello. I'm fine. Today's Sunday. I went to church. Hope everything's well. Goodbye." That's all I ever wrote on a card. The first card my family got from me was the one I sent to my mother. Marcie was right there, too. I knew if mama got it, then Marcie would get it too.

I knew a kid who worked in the *loge* or post office. They called it the *vorloge*. If the German guards wanted to take somebody's cigarettes, they took them out of the package. When they opened up my packages from Marcie, they kept one of the pictures. This kid brought it in for me hidden in his shirt and gave it to me.

> Monday Nov 13, 1944 — "Another new week and I wonder what it will bring. If I just get a letter or two from Marcie and Terry this week I will be well satisfied. Have two letters so far and they are about worn out from reading them so often. Had quite a busy day, did a big washing."

> Nov 20, 1944 — "Today has been a happy one for me. Received three letters and one of them had a picture of our little son and his grandma and grandpa. Was

also glad to hear from my sweet little wife."

Nov 21, 1944 — "Got letter from my darling and they are having more news in them each time."

* * * * *

Father (Capt.) T.J.E. Lynch was a Catholic priest in the British Army at the prison camp who had been captured in Africa. He had gotten malaria somewhere and was now bald. He said Mass and heard confessions for us even though he wasn't in our compound. He rotated between the American and English compounds in the four lagers. There were always guards in the back of the room when he said Mass. Once I saw out of the corner of my eye when one of the guards made the sign of the cross. He must have been a Catholic, too. He had to do it secretly because he watched so the other guards wouldn't see him do it.

Someone was always on hand to lead the Rosary. Usually it was Bill Wixtel. He always led the rosary – always. He helped Father Lynch serve Mass. We had Rosary every evening followed by the Litany of the Blessed Virgin, prayers for peace, the *De Profundus*, and the prayer of contrition. I went as often as I could. I was glad that I had my rosary with me all the time since D-Day.

Nov 17, 44 — "Went to Mass this morning and did a little washing afterwards. I seem to think of Marcia and Terry and home so much more when I go to Mass."

Sunday Nov 12, 44 — "After roll call I went to Mass which was at 9:50. Father gave a very interesting sermon as he usually does. I enjoy hearing him. We went to the Red Cross room this afternoon and listened to the phonograph. Got some new records and it was enjoyed by all."

Bill Wixtel was one of the faithful who went to Mass and evening Rosary. He wrote in the *Wartime Log* a note to me and a prayer:

> "O God, the Maker and Creator of all things, look down upon me, Thy humble servant with tender pity and hear the prayer of one who loves You. Have mercy on all my comrades who have gone before Thee for judgement. Grant that they may not languish in the pain of purgatory, but in Thy justice and mercy

Hand drawing of the Blessed Virgin Mary.
(Source: *A Wartime Log*)

pardon them of their offenses and bring them to Thee for all eternity in Thy everlasting home. Amen. Eternal rest give unto them, O Lord, and let the perpetual light shine upon them. May they rest in peace. Amen."

* * * * *

We celebrated events that were taking place at home. We voted on the first Tuesday of November, we had Thanksgiving, and we had Christmas.

Nov 7, 44 — "Today is election day back in the states. All of us fellows voted here for the fun of it and Roosevelt won by a landslide. Wonder how long it will be before we do find out."

Nov 11, 44 — "We heard that Roosevelt was reelected."

Thanksgiving, Nov 30, 1944 — "Even though I am in a Kriege camp, I have a lot to be thankful for. Especially to have heard from my sweet little family and to know that they are all well and happy. I am well and getting along O.K. We had a little thanksgiving show this afternoon and this evening sixteen of us had a little party. The main topic was that we missed our families and our homes."

Dec 24, 1944 — "Terry boy's birthday. Especially today I have been thinking of Terry and his Mother. Wish I could be with you and celebrate Terry's birthday and have some of his cake. Hope to be with you on this next one. Hear there is going to be mail call tonight so maybe I'll be lucky enough to get a letter on his birthday."

Christmas Eve, Dec 24, 1944 — "First I went to Mass this morning, and after Mass we had our Red Cross Xmas parcel in our rooms ready for us to open. It comes as much fun for me to open it as it must have been for Terry on Xmas eve. It was a wonderful parcel and many nice things that I will list on another page. From 3:00 until 4:30 p.m. our barracks went to the Xmas show. It was really a swell show. Made me lonesome and homesick. Think I will feel that way a lot during the holiday season."

Xmas day, Dec 25, 1944 — "We couldn't have Midnight Mass, but we had it at 10:00 this morning. The choir sang swell this morning. After Mass, 'Art, my combine partner' and I fixed a nice Xmas dinner much better than I thought we would have. Had Jerry Pea soup, turkey, spuds, bread, butter, jam, plum pudding, coffee, candy, and nuts. It didn't compare with any of Marcie's or Mom's holiday dinners but it was nice in Kriege land. This afternoon I wrote two cards one to Marcie and Terry and to Mom and Dad. This evening Fisher invited me over to his room and we had ice cream and cake. It was delicious, the first I had as a POW. We also had a swell little party last night in barracks nine in the washroom. The fellows there are really swell and I'll always remember them. May God bless you all at home."

Jan 1, 1945 — "May 1945 bring me much closer to Marcy and Terry and may it be very soon. We had a very nice New Years show today and made me a little more lonesome and homesick than usual."

* * * * *

The Krauts – the German guards were in a barracks a little ways from ours. Every morning at 5:00 and 5:30, we could hear them sing. They all sang together – really good singing. Those German guards knew how to sing. They were all just young guys. Some of them had been in the States and spoke good English. They came back to Germany, but weren't in the regular army. They were here with us.

I talked a little bit with one of the guards. When the

Cartoon of Thanksgiving dinner at Stalag Luft IV.
(Source: *A Wartime Log*)

soles of my boots were worn out, he took them into town and had them repaired for me. Those were the same boots I wore all the way on the long march. I still have them.

> Jan 9, 1945 — "Had my boots fixed today, leather soles and rubber heels. They done a swell job, but I didn't think I would get them repaired for the first time in a POW camp. We had quite a snow fall off and on this past week. It is almost all gone now."

Sometimes the guards got angry at us. If the Allies were coming along a little better in the war and gaining ground, they'd wake us up two or three o'clock in the morning when it was pitch dark. All the lights had been turned off outside of the compound area. We didn't turn the lights on or off because they did all that someplace else. Then they'd turn on all of the lights at two o'clock in the morning. They came with about 10 or 20 guards into one of the barracks and just holler like hell. They'd wake everybody up if they were asleep. They'd say, "Heraus mit din!" and "Get up!" We'd all get up. Then they threw everything we had on the floor. If we were wearing anything, we had to throw it on the pile on the floor. They'd get mad and tip over the beds and even throw them on the floor. Then they stomped out of the room, closed the door, and turned out all the lights. We'd have to just live with ourselves until morning because we couldn't see anything. Shutters were on the window, so we couldn't see even if the moon was out.

The guards did that because something had happened. It didn't have to happen in the camp. It might have happened over in Belgium, Russia, or someplace like that. They got mad because they were being punished because of it, too.

* * * * *

Hand drawing of a Kriege room at Stalag Luft IV by Howard Farr.

(Source: *A Wartime Log*)

Every once in a while a Gestapo came to the camp with his big black coat and big black hat. He raised a ruckus with everything. He'd find something wrong, no matter what it was. He just stormed around mad, got in his big black car, and stormed out with his big boots.

* * * * *

Hand drawing of a Kreige room at Stalag Luft IV ready for the holiday season by Howard Farr.

(Source: *A Wartime Log*)

6. The Long March

We could tell that there was a lot of movement in other parts of the camp during the first couple days in February 1945. We heard different things from the guards. I tried to get a little information, but I never knew what was true and what wasn't. It really surprised me when they told us that we were going to leave the camp the next day, February 6th. They didn't say why, but we just assumed that the Russians were getting very close. They didn't want the Russians to get us, and they didn't want to be captured by the Russians either. They thought that if they took us, that would keep them from getting captured or killed by the Russians. They got us out of there before the Russians got to the camp, and that's why we went.

There were some who went two days ahead of us. We didn't know that a whole column of other prisoners in another compound left because you couldn't see those compounds. They went out of their gate, but we couldn't see it. We had to go out of our gate the other way, but they couldn't see it either. The gates went in different directions. We couldn't crawl up in the tower and see anything or get up on a fence. We were just flat on the ground so that's all we could see.

We went out between 7:00 and 9:00 in the morning of February 6th when it was still dark. We marched due west about 30 kilometers to the little town of Standelin that first day. It seemed like a hell of a long walk that first day and we camped near a lake. On February 7th we marched 24 km to Morterlietz. We went 24 km as we marched thru Stolzberg, Fietlow, Petershagen, Roman, and Koslin on February 8th. The next day we just stayed there for some reason and never really knew why.

On February 10th we marched 24 km across country. We went 30 km the next day across country and over back roads. We walked 6 km thru Stuchow and Kummin on the 12th. We marched 36 km on the 13th, and went through Wollin. We slept in fields that night 6 km from Swinemünde right along the Baltic Sea. The next day we received one-fifth of an American Red Cross food parcel. We passed through Swinemünde and crossed the Oder River at 11:00 a.m. That was a 20 km march. From there we went through Usedom and stopped 10 km from Anklam, having covered 28 km that day. We rested February 16th, 17th, and 18th. At least we were supposed to rest. It was always too cold to rest.

We started out again on February 19th and marched 22 km. We passed within 1 km to the north of Anklam. We were delayed on the 20th, but marched 12 km on the 21st. We marched 14 km on the 22nd and went through Jarman. We went through Demmin on the 23rd having marched 26 km. On February 24th, we marched 24 km through Stavenhagen. We rested on the 25th as we waited for a so-called transport. We rested on February 26th through March 2nd. We received one Red Cross parcel on March 1st. We never had enough to eat during the march. When you don't have enough to eat, all you do is think about food and talk about food.

We used the cigarettes in the Red Cross parcels to trade for food with farmers whose land we crossed. We weren't supposed to do that, and we'd get in trouble with the guards if they caught us trading.

The next day we went 22 km south. We marched 24 km on the 4th and went through Waren, which is on the north side of a lake. On the 5th, we went 28 km to Malchow and another 25 km the next day as we went through Karow. We rested on March 7th.

On March 8th we walked 14 km. We marched 16 km the next day as we passed through Malchim. We rested on

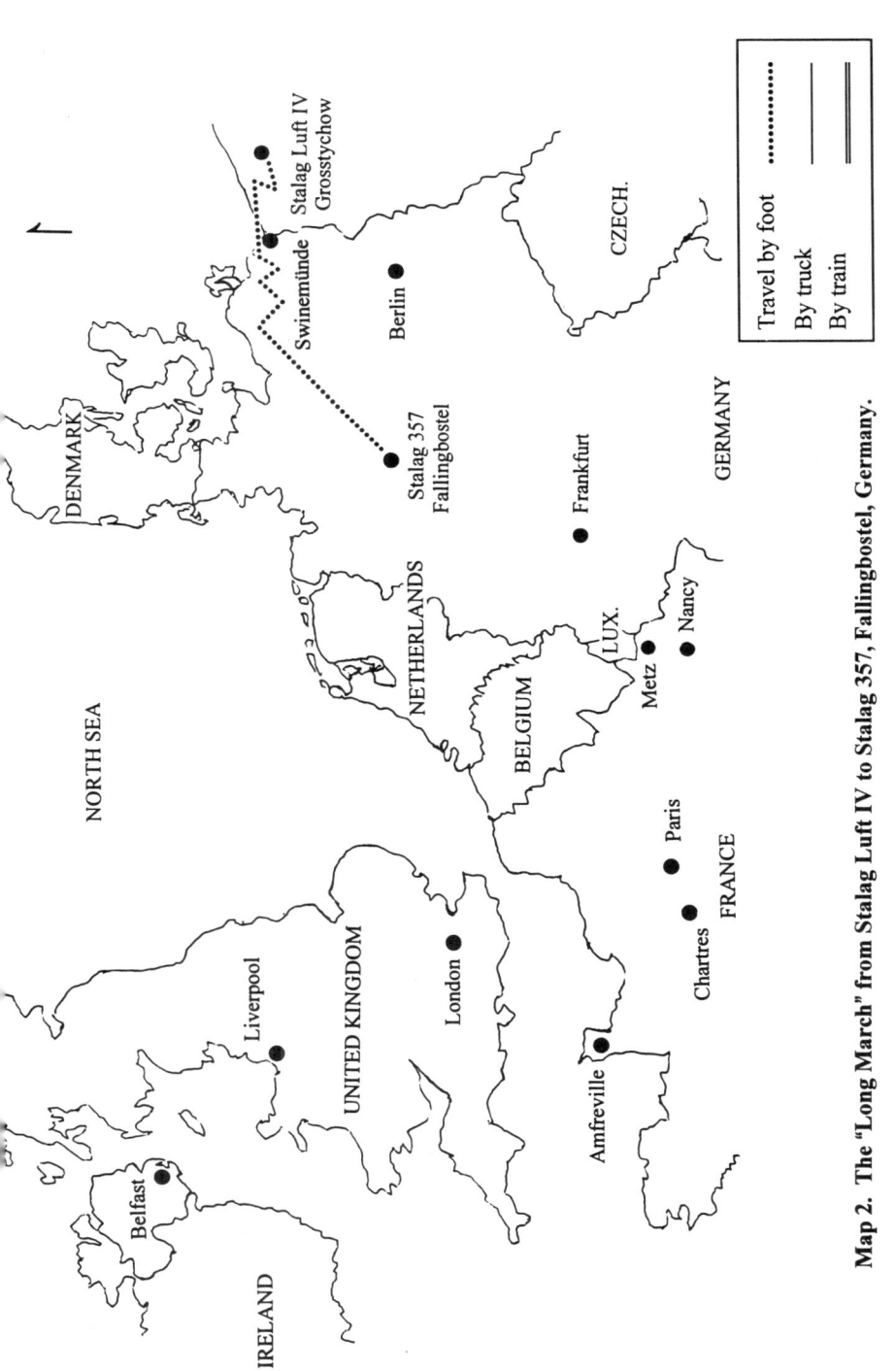

Map 2. The "Long March" from Stalag Luft IV to Stalag 357, Fallingbostel, Germany.

the 10th through the 13th as we waited for transport. We started off again on March 13th and went 20 km through Lübz. We went 22 km on the 14th and marched through Parchim next to a river. We rested on March 15th through18th at Neese which is near Ludwigslust. This was supposedly our destination.

We started marching again on March 19th and went 23 km through Grabow. We marched another 23 km on the 20th, 19 km on the 21st, and 23 km on the 22nd. We received half of a Red Cross parcel that day and rested on the 23rd. We had almost nothing to eat during the whole march. Sometimes we had a little Red Cross food, and the Germans gave us a few potatoes. The next day we marched 15 km through Bevensen, and another 14 km on the 25th. We rested on the 26th and 27th.

On March 28th, we marched 4 km to a train at Ebstorf. We rode that train to Fallisbostel and walked four more km on March 29th from the train to Stalag 357 and XI-B. We marched a total of 625 km between February 6th and March 29th.

* * * * *

I kept my *Wartime Log* with me during the whole march. I carried it under my clothes against my belly. No matter what happened, I wanted to be sure to save the book. Howard kept track of what we did and where we were all the time. He saw road signs and wrote them on little scraps of paper. Later when we were in England in the hospital, he wrote them down in this book.

Howard Farr, Art Schwegert, and I slept near each other and were together constantly. We walked together or looked for each other all the time. We always kept track of where the other ones were. If I knew where there was some grain, I told them to go through a door and around the corner to find it. If they knew where there was some barley or something they'd do the same for me. We'd fill our pockets at night in the barn, then we'd have something to chew the next day. We'd always tell the other guy where to go to get it, so he'd get his pockets full before the German guards quit letting us walk in there. We'd walk into the granary like we had to go to the bathroom and fill up our pockets. Oats were hard to chew, but barley was a lot better.

Not many of the guards spoke English. We had two or three guys who spoke fluent German. They were gunners, just like many of the men. I knew a couple of them. I always wished I knew them well enough to have been with them. They seemed to know what was going on because they spoke German. The Germans wanted to hang on to those guys because they could communicate with all of us that way. They were closer to the guards with everything. They got a little more food and a little bit better deal where to sleep. They slept where the hay was a little bit better, and things like that.

* * * * *

We were out in a field one time and it was terribly cold. The Germans had picked up a shovel at a farm. They made us dig a latrine about two feet by three feet out in the field where we were going to be that night. We had the latrine so we'd all go in the same spot. They didn't want feces all over the field, I guess. When we were in a farm yard, they didn't really care where we'd go. After digging the latrine, they put a piece of tree across it and fastened it down. It wasn't anything fancy.

They said that only one of us should get on it at a time. If two or three got on it at the same time, the whole thing could break because it wasn't that strong. A person could fall or slip into the hole because there was snow on the ground. Later that evening, a guy went to the latrine and the thing broke. He fell in and then stood up in it. He was covered face and all. They pushed a stick down in there and pulled him out. The hole wasn't very deep, but it was deep enough that he had to be pulled out. They grabbed one of his hands and then his other hand to got him out. They took all of his clothes off of him. The Germans didn't even think of helping. Whatever happened to him happened. We had to take care of ourselves. They put all his clothes on the snow and dirt, and tried to beat them on the ground to get the feces out. They dried it as good as they could even though there wasn't a fire around. Then he put his clothes back on again. Everyone who had helped him stunk just like him.

* * * * *

The German general who was the head officer on that march rode a bicycle in front of us. He didn't have a car or a horse or wagon. A horse and wagon followed us to pick up those whose feet got frozen and they couldn't walk anymore. He went ahead of us two or three miles to find an open spot to sleep for the night. Then, when we arrived they ran all of us into part of the barn for the night. We were able to warm up a little each night if we could keep the barn warm with a little hay. It was a hell of a lot better than sleeping out in the open field. We couldn't build a fire out in the open field because the Allied airplanes might drop a bomb on one little fire. They had a habit of doing that all the time.

We walked and walked. The wagon picked up more guys the further we walked. Sometimes we'd lose a horse and wagon because the horses didn't want to go anymore. They were tired or whoever owned the horses had to take them back. Then they found another two horses and went on some more. I never wanted to get on that wagon if I didn't have to because I didn't want to freeze on that thing. I wanted to try to keep walking as much as I could.

It was incredibly cold during the march. Several people froze their hands, feet, legs, and faces. Some people lost their limbs because of frostbite. Both of Art Schwegert's feet froze during the march, and that's probably why he got separated from Howard Farr and me half way through the march. If people got too cold, they could get on the horse-drawn wagon. I didn't want to do that because you get even colder if you don't keep moving.

* * * * *

Before D-Day, the officers told us that if we got captured we would be a detriment to the Germans. They always had to take some soldiers away from the front lines to guard us. Then we'd be a detriment to them. While we were on that march, we'd say to each other, "Get along as well as you can and you'll have a chance at getting home." I hoped and prayed that would come true. I did get home, and I was lucky that I did. A lot of them didn't.

* * * * *

We walked right by where the V-bombs went off. We could see them on concrete pads. The guards told us that if we got off that road at any time, they'd shoot us no matter what we did. We knew when we were going by the V-bombs because they didn't want any sabotage there. They didn't want anyone to get in there and blow up anything.

I saw the Germans just shoot a guy and I wondered what they shot him for. It could have been because he was shitting in the wrong place or he hollered back at them. Nobody knows.

We got to Stalag 357 near Fallingbostel March 29th, 1945, just around Easter time. Fallingbostel was in a small town between two prison camps, Stalag 357 and Stalag Luft XI-B. They were only about a half mile apart from each other, and we were in and out of both of them. I don't know who had been in those camps before we got there, except it looked like it must have been men from about every country. They were pushing everybody in there. When they were full, I'd imagine that there must have been between 30,000 and 35,000 men in there at one time.

We were in there less than two weeks before they

started to root us all out again to go back across the Elbe River. The Germans started to evacuate Lager R and part of Lager C of Stalag 357 on April 6th. They evacuated the rest of Lagers A, B, and C on the 7th and 8th. Russian POWs arrived on April 9th. The next day, I received one-half of a Red Cross parcel. About 1,500 Kriegies returned to Lagers A and B on April 11th.

We had just come across the Elbe, and now they wanted us to go back across it again. I couldn't imagine getting back out on the road again.

I said, "Howard, let's just stay here." So we just stayed there in the camp. We hid under a big Red Cross box until, as we hoped, everyone was gone.

7. Liberated

In mid-April 1945, we knew that Montgomery's British forces were coming by listening to what was being said mouth-to-mouth. We heard the guns and watched the dog fights everyday. A couple days later, they strafed our barracks. The tracers came down and set some of our barracks on fire. The shells burned down two or three of them, and two men didn't get out.

We were there all day as the fighting was going on. We watched the Messerschmitts have dogfights with the P-38s or P-47s. I watched when somebody got shot down and jumped out with a parachute. He came down and was put into the camp. I tried to get next to him to find out what was happening. He told me a little bit, but he didn't know that much either because he had just flown out of some air field in France.

We dug trenches to stay in. I never slept inside of the barracks. They were too full of lice and fleas, and were so filled with every kind of nationality imaginable that I never went back into the barracks to sleep. I just slept on the ground, a fox hole, or a ditch out in front of the barracks. These were all inside the camp's fence.

More Jerry rations came to the camp on April 13th and 15th. But by then, almost all of the prisoners had been evacuated by the Germans. During the evacuation, Howard Farr and I hid under a large Red Cross box in the middle of the compound so we wouldn't have to go. There might have been a couple other men who hid like Howard and I did because there were only about 80 or 90 of us left. About 70 or 80 men in the hospital also were left behind as the Germans evacuated. We stayed right in the camp because we knew the spearhead was coming with Montgomery and his troops.

After the airplanes were gone, we were still in the camp. Tanks went past our prison camp during the night. Then on the morning of April 16th, 1945, more tanks started to come through. They didn't stop or come in the camp. They didn't think about us being in the camp any more than they thought about Uncle Sam being in the camp. They just rolled on by. We could hear the tanks, trucks, and

Fred Peschl and friends by a guard tower at Stalag 357.

everything going by as the British with General Montgomery went on their way.

I don't think the German guards stayed in the towers. They all left. The Germans were the first ones who wanted to get out of there when Montgomery was coming. They wanted us to go with them. But we didn't go. The men who were in the hospital just stayed there. I don't think anybody slept in the hospital as far as I could tell.

Howard and I hid under a large Red Cross box right in the middle of the prison camp compound. We didn't know why the British were all leaving. We didn't know why we stayed, except that I didn't want to get on the road again. Howard didn't either, so we agreed to stay.

The British Army didn't stop because they had one objective – to keep on going to the war front. We were just a side deal that happened to be in the way. That went on a whole day and night. At 11 o'clock the next morning on April 16th, one British tank came into the camp. They said we were officially liberated. The first thing we thought about was getting something to eat. They said they weren't going to give us very much to eat. They gave us some tea and crumpets. Nobody was going to get a meal, and nobody was to leave the camp. We were to stay right there.

> April 16, 1945 — "FREEDOM This morning at 11:00 a.m. the gates were opened to a British armored division and the tanks, armored cars, and jeeps, rolled in. They were the 'Desert Rats,' one of Montgomery's famous division coming from the Bremen and Hamburg area. I was so happy after 10 months and 6 days of German prison camps that I ran, shouted aloud, and even tears came to my eyes. I knew then that I shouldn't be too long before I could meet my little son, his mother, and Mother and Dad. I will always say a prayer of thankfulness to

Almighty God for this happy day. It will be a happier one when I return home."

* * * * *

Somebody told us that they were going to send in English personnel clerks and maybe a few U.S. Army people to take care us. They wanted to know who we were and what outfit we were with. Howard Farr and I were together, but we didn't know where our friend Art Schwegert was. We found out later that he was in a hospital someplace after the long march because he had gotten a bad frost bite. He got back home to the States later on. After that, they told us that we were going to be there at Stalag 357 for just a couple more days.

They set up a camp for the personnel clerks and us outside of the barracks. The barracks were so filthy dirty and full of lice and fleas that they didn't want to be in the barracks. We all stayed outside and they worked out of a truck with a canvas over it.

When I was still in Stalag 357 on April 19th, 1945, the English personnel clerks let us write cards home. I wrote to Marcie and Terry:

"April 19th, 1945. My sweet darling and Terry boy, I am no longer a POW and I am now under our own Army, which I'm very, very thankful for. This Camp 357 was taken over by a British division April 16 at 11:00 a.m. It was a wonderful feeling to see our tanks, cars, jeeps, and etc. come rolling into the camp after so many months. I am not in the same camp I was a few months ago. We are living on a percentage basis, so sweetheart, I am now waiting my turn. Can't tell you anything definite as to when I will be back to the States, but we think we may go to England or France first. I am just fine, and have had my first white bread in almost a year. I'm really looking forward to meeting our little son and his mother, as well. Tell mother and dad I hope to have her fried chicken and raisin bread on my birthday. All my love and kisses. May God bless and keep you, Fred."

We drew straws to see when we would get to leave the camp. I drew a straw to leave the fourth day, and Howard drew one to leave the ninth or tenth day. There were only between six to 10 men who could go each day. Between 80 and 100 of us were rounded up at the camp and hospital to return to England. The wounded and other men in the hospital went first, then we could go. They could only take what there was room for after the airplane was full of wounded. That's how they did it, but I didn't know all that until the third day.

After Howard and I drew straws to see when we'd leave, I said, "I kinda hate to go without you, Howard."

He said, "I wish you would stay, too." I traded my turn with a guy who was going later so I could go with Howard. I was really glad that I stayed because the plane that I would have been on got shot down over the Rhine. I don't know why that happened. I'm lucky to be here.

We were at the camp for 10 more days. I went out of the camp by myself and got a couple of chickens and brought them in. We cleaned, cooked, and ate them, even though they told us not to. We still did it. I found an abandoned blacksmith forge at to cook them on.

I went to the barracks and collected some of the junk that was left in there -- things like a belt, bullets, insignia, and a big poster. I just picked them up and took them. I stuffed them in a bag along with my box. I also found a box camera with film in it that must have been left by one of the German guards. I asked some of the men at the camp to take pictures of Howard, men I knew, and me with that camera.

Fred Peschl with chickens (lower left) and Howard Farr (top, second from right)

When it was Howard's and my turn to leave on April 23rd, we crossed over the Elbe River by truck. Later we went across the Rhine River to get to the landing strip. They used the landing strip to bring supplies over and take the wounded back. They went back and forth and back and forth, and the war was still going on beyond us. As we crossed the river, I looked out of the back end of the truck and wondered where we were going. I really thought that we were going to go to Lucky Strike, a rest camp in France close to Belgium or Holland where they used to give furloughs. Then I thought that we'd go to Le Havre, France and return in a ship from there. But instead, the plane turned and went toward England. We landed in Oxford, England.

* * * * *

We went to the hospital in Oxford, England. They checked us outside of the hospital by asking who we were,

Fred Peschl and Howard Farr at Stalag 357.

our names, and things like that. They gave us tags with our names on them. The tags told us where we were supposed to go when we went inside the hospital. We had to take off all our clothes so they could burn them outside the hospital. We threw our clothes on a pile in a big open spot on the ground and watched them burn. They burned everything including our clothes and shoes.

I asked one of the men who told us to take off our clothes, "Could I keep these boots?"

He said, "I don't think you'd better because we're burning all the shoes."

"I really would like to keep these," I said, "These are the only things I've got."

He said, "OK." I kept my book, of course, my boots, rosary, and other things like the photos, bullets, and insignia I got at Stalag 357. I had those with me in a sack. I put them with the boots. I had the film from the camera, but had thrown away the square box camera because I didn't have anymore film.

The song that was popular when we got back to England was Roy Rogers (or somebody like that) singing "Don't Fence Me In." I had just gotten out of the fence. I'll never forget when they played "Don't Fence Me In" during my hospital stay.

I was in the hospital about a week and felt pretty good. They fed me only so much for each meal. It was about the fourth day that I could go to the mess hall to eat. I was down to less than 130 pounds when I was in the hospital. I weighed about 135 when I got back to the United States, but I had weighed over 155 pounds when I jumped on D-Day.

* * * *

I still had some of my personal things back at Tollerton Hall. There was a radio I had bought in Ireland. I learned in Ireland that if I put a light bulb between the wires to cut down the current, the radio worked good. I also had a bike in my room. There were things that Marcie and others sent to me. Joe Poplawski had put all these things in a box for me after D-Day. Joe was back in England and stayed there until the end of July. He fixed a footlocker or box for all my things that were still in Tollerton Hall and sent it to Marcie. They sent all the stuff back for everybody. That must have been a big job. Of the 2,200 men in the 507th who jumped on D-Day, there were only 847 men who made it back. All the rest of them were either killed, wounded, or captured. Some of them went to the hospital and then went back to unit again; some never went back to the unit; some went home.

Marcie also got a letter or two from England from Father Lynch. I know that she answered them.

There was something not just right with Howard Farr when we were in the hospital in England. That's why he had to stay behind, and I went on ahead. Howard and I talked about getting killed and not getting to go home. We said, "Well, if we're still both here tomorrow, we'll be together. We'll take care of one another as long as we're together." We did that right up to the end. Even when he never left that hospital in England and I did, he felt real bad about it. I felt bad, too, because I was going home without him. I got to see his mother and dad when I got back to the U.S. I was so glad when he finally got back. We though a lot about questions like, "Why did I come back? Why didn't some of the others come back?" I still think in my mind that God had something for me to do or finish whatever it might be. That's why I'm here.

* * * * *

One day they said we were going to London, so I figured I'd go to. I thought we'd be there a little while, then get out and go home. Instead we went to London and went out to see the sights. I went to a dance one night at

Piccadilly. I saw Howard Nielson there. He was a big football player from Yankton. Nielson flew across the Channel and checked for places to land planes. (He's in Tom Brokaw's book about people in World War II). I remember getting drunk. I never drank any whiskey after that again. I stayed out all night. I don't know why I did that, but I did. We came home with a guy who was driving a horse and wagon in the fog. He took us "home," which was back to some billets. They were old hotels used for billets.

I borrowed $5 or a Pound or two of English money from the Red Cross to have something to spend. I paid it back right away. The Red Cross was really good to me. I couldn't say a bad thing about it. When I was in England and just wanted to borrow a few bucks, they were right there to help me. When we first got off the boat in Liverpool from the U.S., I was so sick. I got off the boat and had a cup of coffee and a donut at Liverpool. It was the best thing I ate since I left the States. That cup of coffee and donut tasted like you wouldn't believe. I said I'd never forget the Red Cross.

We wondered why we were so long in London. Everyday we got questioned about a lot of things. I thought there was something wrong when they asked, "Where did you live?" or "What did you do?" Then they started all over. Every morning when some American clerks got done questioning us, they started to ask us more questions like: "Who's Alley Oop?", "Who is Andy Gump?", "Who is Babe Ruth?", "Who were the Browns?", or "Who were the Cardinals?" I knew the Cardinals and the Browns were St. Louis. Andy Gump and Alley Oop were in the funny papers. Why did they want to know all this? We asked, but we never got any response. We were there about 10 days and they questioned us everyday. The more questions we answered and they didn't get what they wanted, the longer we stayed. Finally they told us. When we left Camp 357, some Germans came back with us in American uniforms. Some of the Germans found American uniforms and dressed up in them. They fit perfectly. There were lots of uniforms laying around so they made sure they found uniforms that fit. After they put on those uniforms, they came in among us. Those Germans took an American name and came along with us when we went back to England. They must have been in the States before the war and knew more about the States than we did. Maybe they went to school in Chicago, Atlanta, or someplace. Their parents in Germany were rich and had enough money to send them to school in the States. They didn't really follow the funnies or baseball, so they were using those kinds of questions to catch them. If they couldn't answer these questions, they kept them. They were just trying to escape Germany because they wanted to go back to America with the Americans and start over rather than stay in Germany. That's what we finally found out they were doing.

* * * * *

After we got all that settled, we were on our way down to Plymouth, England. I thought they'd take the whole bunch of us down there, but they only took a couple bus loads of us, like a hundred at a time. I thought we'd have a great big boat to get on. Instead, we got on an LST, about 110 of us on each LST. An LST is a landing craft where the tanks were down underneath. A big door opened in the front for soldiers to hit the beach and tanks would roll out. When we were on them, the Navy hung their clothes down there when they washed them. There was a lot of room. There were 18 LSTs that were to leave at the same time. We got there and had to wait a few more days to fill all of the LSTs. Once we left England, we went to the Azores, across the Atlantic Ocean further south, and came up by Florida.

It took us 18 days to get across the ocean. It usually took 12 days for mail to get across the ocean from England. We went very fast, as far as that goes, because we came home on LSTs that took 18 or 19 days. Luckily the weather was calm. I pealed potatoes on deck and listened to the radio everyday. There were about 100 Navy guys and 110 of us on each LST. There weren't any tanks on the bottom of the LSTs to make them heavy. They just left all the tanks over in Europe. I wonder what they did with all them? A lot of scrap iron, I guess.

We got ahead of a hurricane and got into Chesapeake Bay at Newport News, Virginia. Two or three of the 18 ships were quarantined because of some kind of sickness. Ours wasn't quarantined, but the others had to stay out there two more weeks.

We left England on June 6, 1945, and arrived at Camp Patrick Henry, Virginia on June 22nd. We went to the barracks and were fed and treated very well. We were there several days and they learned all they could about us. I knew the ropes about getting to the commissary and supply. So I went to Supply and got a brand new jump suit and uniform. I needed a new uniform because my uniform had been back in England and got sent back in the States after D-Day.

* * * * *

The war in Europe ended on May 8th, 1945.

* * * * *

8. Home Again

I was at Camp Patrick Henry, Virginia for only a few days in late June1945, then got on a troop train. I told Howard Farr when I left Oxford, England that I'd stop in Chicago to visit his parents. I figured I'd take a train home and would stop in Chicago and Minneapolis. That's what happened. I rode a troop train on my way to Fort Snelling in St. Paul, Minnesota. We stopped in Chicago and I called Howard's folks with the phone number he gave me. They both came down to Union Station. We visited and cried. I told them, "He'll be coming soon." It was hard to tell them that he wasn't with me. I sure had hoped he'd come home with me.

At that time I didn't know why Howard was left back in England. Later I found out that the reason he was left behind was that he got upset so easily. What he got upset about, I don't know. Whatever it was, he got over it. Later, after he got home and was working in Chicago, we wrote letters to each other and talked on the phone. I used the phone all the time because I was in the meat business. His job was to engineer the bolts that went into the Sears Building. He helped to build the five tallest buildings in Chicago after he got back from the war. He knew what size of bolts were supposed to be used – how long and how big around – for all the windows and every other place in the building. There were many thousands of bolts in those buildings.

About eight or ten years after Howard got home, I went to Chicago for a meat business convention. I called Howard and he came to my hotel. He said, "I'll bring my wife and we'll go up and see some of the buildings that I've helped build."

We ate in the top floor of one of those brand new buildings. We saw pictures of the Presidents on the wall up there.

Howard lived out in Maywood earlier. Now he lives closer to Chicago. I've seen him quite often since then. He and his wife have visited us in DeSmet as well. We really stayed together. You never forget a guy like that.

* * * * *

I arrived at Ft. Snelling on the troop train toward the end of May 1946. We ate on the train in the Army mess kitchen and just kept going. I didn't want to get discharged yet, but wanted to get a furlough first. I received a 70-day furlough at Ft. Snelling. Marcie and Terry were already in Minneapolis to meet me. That's where we first saw each other again. We stayed at the Andrews Hotel in Minneapolis. It cost $6.11 for two days – $2.50 the first day and $3.50 the second. Marcie stayed there one night before I got there. She knew about when I was going to get to Ft. Snelling on the troop train. When I came over from Fort Snelling, Marcie and Terry came downstairs from the room and we met them in the lobby. The first thing Terry wanted was for me to take off my boots so he could put them on. He was about 18 months old. The next day we took a train and went to Yankton where I saw my folks.

We arrived in Yankton in time for my birthday, which was May 24th. Then I started my 70-day furlough. I spent three or four days in the apartment with Marcie and Terry getting reacquainted with them. Then, the first thing I did was to go to work at the meat market. I was getting $18 a week when I left the meat market for Europe. When I came home, the same guy owned the meat market, and he said he'd pay me $40 a week. This was my furlough; I worked the whole furlough. I just wanted to get back to work as soon as I could. I was still in the service and wasn't discharged yet.

I didn't know when I would get discharged, but I

watched my points all the time. I wondered if I had enough points to get out of the service. We had to have 120 points to get out. They were based on how long we were in the service. Our rank had a little bit to do with it. I had two Battle Stars, and that was the big thing. I think I had more than 120 points because I had the two Battle Stars. I never wanted to go over to Japan. They said that's where they were going to go next, and I knew I didn't want that.

After my furlough was done, they sent me down to Hot Springs, Arkansas for two weeks of R-and-R or rehabilitation. I had to see about my health and find out what they were going to do with me. They didn't know what they were going to do with me either. While I was in Hot Springs, they checked everything. The dentist down there happened to own the farm that Marcie and her folks lived on in Menominee, Nebraska. Marcie didn't go with me to Hot Springs. I went alone and lived in a hotel there. She wasn't able to go with me because she and Terry couldn't stay in the same spot that I was. I got a letter from the Army that said:

> Notice to Returnee, August 1945: As for accommodations for your son, Hot Springs will accept your wife only. No other dependents can be accommodated. Her stay cost about $25 for rooms and meals. The government will furnish transportation to Hot Springs only for you. Consequently, your wife will have to pay her own way there and back home.

I received a Battle Stars because I had jumped at Normandy on D-Day. I didn't know that I was supposed to get another one until I was in Hot Springs. They asked, "Where were you when you left Germany?"

I answered, "I was in 357 Prison Camp when Montgomery spearheaded through there."

"Oh, you were in there when they were spearheading through."

I said, "I didn't even have a gun in my hand."

"That's alright," they said, "You get a Battle Star for being there during that time." So, see how I lucked out with that?

I found out in Hot Springs that I had enough points to get out of the service. That was the big thing. Once I knew that, I pushed right away to see if I couldn't just get out. They said, "Yes, you're 10 points over. So you can get out." They made arrangements for me to go from there by train to Camp McCoy, Wisconsin, so I went to Camp McCoy to get discharged.

It was about 5:30 in the afternoon of September 29th, 1945 when I received my discharge papers at Camp McCoy. There weren't any more trains leaving that evening. Camp McCoy is out in the boondocks, and you have to drive all the way down to Sparta, Wisconsin to get on the train. I slept on the floor of the railroad station all night. I got on the early train at 6:00 in the morning and came to Minneapolis and then to Yankton.

* * * * *

Do you remember that watch that the Germans took from me when I was captured? I tried to get reimbursed for it. I filled out a form that reads:

> "Fred Peschl. I was a member of the 507th Parachute Infantry attached to the 82nd Division and was captured in Amperville, France in Normandy on June 10th. My job was jeep driver and scout for the CO. While on patrol one morning at about 3 a.m., I was surrounded and captured by the Germans. My personal wrist watch was taken from me by them at that time and they did not give me any kind of receipt whatsoever. I cannot give a good description of the German, however Col. G.V. Millett, whose address in now 4th Infantry Regiment, Ft. Benning, GA knows of my possessing this watch and also my loss. I was

encouraged to take this watch with me because of the nature of my job. It was a Swiss make, 15 jewel, waterproof and shock proof. This watch is all I am making claim for. The value of the watch was about $30. I was liberated 16 April 1945 by the British troops from Stalag 11-B and 357."

9. Life Goes On

I went to work right away in the same meat market in Yankton that I worked at before the war. Things were going along fine. I tried to make a few extra bucks, but I knew I didn't want to go back to the meat market for the rest of my life. I wanted to go out and do something on my own. I was making plenty of money, but I wasn't doing anything with my life. I wanted to get into my own business. I knew the meat business, so that's what I wanted to do.

I started looking at advertisements in the *Sioux City Journal*, and found one for a bread truck driver. They wanted people who owned their own trucks, and would buy bread from the Wonder Bread company and resell it. They'd make their own route, as big a route as they could make. I thought about that as a possibility. Then I saw an advertisement for a locker plant for sale in DeSmet, South Dakota. It had just been built and was brand new. Just built, brand new – that's what struck me the most. I contacted the *Sioux City Journal* to get the telephone number to call. I called and talked with Harry Egan, who was selling the locker plant for Whitey Sorenson. Harry was an attorney in DeSmet.

Whitey Sorenson was already out of the Navy. He had been in Japan and built things for the Navy. He was smart enough to know that he could borrow money from the government to build a locker plant, and not use a nickel of his own money, which he didn't have. He didn't know how to butcher, but he did know how to build. He built the plant and put refrigeration in it. He bought a little saw, a grinder, and some of the basic things – not a whole lot, but the basic things. He rented 150 lockers to farmers, and collected money from them at about $10 apiece. He had that money, then he advertised the locker. I saw the ad, so I jumped in my Model-A, which I bought for $110 when I came home from the Army. I had sold my Model-T before I left. I also owned an older Chevy, which I stored while I was gone. I sold that while I was in the Army.

I came to DeSmet and looked at the plant. It looked pretty good, so I went over to see Ted Meyers, the banker.

I said, "Ted, if I buy this place, could you loan me some money?"

He said, "You find out what he wants for it, then come over and tell me. We'll see what we can do. I won't say, 'Yes.' or 'No.'"

"I've got to go back today because I'm working," I said, "But I'll be back next Sunday."

I didn't want to miss one day of work. I went back to Yankton down the gravel road. It was gravel all the way to Salem and down Hiway 81. I got home and told my dad about it.

He said, "Where are you going to get the money?"

I said, "Well, I need $10,000. I know that. He wants more, but we'll see what we can do. I don't want to give up on this deal."

I didn't ask him if he had any money because I needed the big amount from the bank first. I knew I couldn't get any out of the bank in Yankton. I couldn't get a dime in Yankton to buy the business. They knew my name, but we never had anything. My dad hadn't put any money in the bank for quite a while because he had $200 in it and they lost it. When you're that old, you don't put money in the bank when they lost $200. He worked in the Post Office. Every bit of the money he got from the Post Office, he used for day-to-day living, and saved a little bit besides.

I drove back to DeSmet the next Sunday and went to talk to Ted Meyers. I went to his house and parked my

Model-A out in front. He was home sick with the flu in the back bedroom of his house.

"Ted, what do you think I should pay for that locker plant?" I asked.

He said, "Well, I know they want more than what they've got in it. You offer him $10,000. I'll give you $7,000."

I thought, "Where in the hell am I going to get the other $3,000?"

I had just received $1,000 in the mail. It was money the Army sent to me as back pay from being in the prison camp. While I was in the camp, Marcie got an allotment for herself and Terry. That gave her a few dollars every month to pay for an apartment while I was gone. She got along just fine on that allotment. She didn't have to work except for babysitting for George B. German. I knew I had $1,000, but I didn't tell that to Ted right away.

I went to back to Yankton to talk to my dad. I asked, "Do you have any money that you could loan me?"

He said, "Yes, how much would you need?"

"Around $1,000," I answered.

"Fred, let's go down in the basement and see what we've got."

We went down in the basement and he pulled back a big slab of cement in the potato room. Underneath it were several one-pound Folgers and Nash coffee cans. There were $10 bills and $5 bills in each can. It came to a total of $1,009.

He said, "I'll give you $1,000. I've got enough." So then I knew I had $2,000. We put them back under the cement.

Later that day, I said to Marcie, "Your sister and brother-in-law are selling their farm. Maybe they've got a little money." I checked with them right away.

"Helen, I've known you a long time," I said. "You know who I am."

"Yes, I know who you are."

So I said, "I know that you're going to be moving to western Nebraska. How much interest are you going to get for your money in the bank?"

She said, "2¢ for each dollar."

I said, "I'll tell you what. If you'll loan me $1,000, I'll give you 3¢."

"Fred, how are you going to pay that back?"

I said, "Helen, of the three that I'm borrowing it from, (I said three, but I was one), I'll pay you first. But I have to pay the bank when that comes due. I'll tell you just like I told the bank. I'm going to get up at 5:00 o'clock each morning and go from farm to farm with my Model-A and a trailer. I'll butcher their animals and cut up the meat right on the farms. We'll get you paid."

She said, "OK." So I got the other $1,000.

Then I came up to DeSmet and paid for the locker plant. I was in business January 9th, 1946 – just right after I got out of the Army. I worked my butt off when I got up there. We lived in one big bedroom of Tex Meyers' grandfather's house.

One thing that Marcie asked me, "Do they have a Catholic church in DeSmet?" She hadn't come up to DeSmet with me yet.

"Yes, they do – St. Thomas Aquinas Catholic Church."

* * * * *

My brother and dad came up with me after I looked at the locker plant the second time. It was brand new and they were doing pheasants – hundreds or thousands a night. They were bringing the pheasants down to the locker just to freeze them. Then the hunters came to get the pheasants and went home.

Those were the good years between the end of World War II and 1960s. We did 2,000 pheasants every night when we got into it. We saved all the feathers. The hunters picked the feathers, but we saved all of them. We had five kinds of feathers, including tail feathers, almonds, and reds under the neck. Almond feathers were worth more, and the tail feathers were good, too. We sold the feathers to buyers in Chicago and New York, and they sold them to people in Japan and China. I knew how to work with those buyers, so that helped a lot. I wouldn't give them anything without the money.

That's how we got into our business. In 1951, we started building our house. It was all because of the pheasants, not because of the meat. We had lots of hunters here. We got the short stop for the St. Louis Cardinals – he'd come up. Different ones from out-of-state came up. They invited me to Florida, and I went down there to watch them play ball. I got to go to two World Series in Milwaukee because they give me tickets.

Then I got into that meat business. It was really good. I knew I had to work with meat, so I started butchering right away. The first year I butchered from farm to farm and brought it into the locker. Then we added on to the locker six times. Every two years Charlie Greer, the undertaker, lent me enough money to add on. He owned the building and was very good to us. We got along great. He liked me and I liked him. He said he would help me, so he built on. It cost me two or three thousand dollars every time we added on. Two years later, I'd add on again. Then I bought the smoke house and then another smoke house. Pretty soon I had four smoke houses.

* * * * *

Terry was only two years old when we moved to DeSmet. Our daughter, Vicki was born February 15th, 1949. She was born in Lake Preston, South Dakota because the hospital in DeSmet hadn't been built yet.

Amy, Terry, and Dianne Peschl (left to right).

We got very active in the community and St. Thomas Aquinas Catholic Church. I joined the Knights of Columbus in DeSmet in 1952.

I conducted a meat school for the FFA in the DeSmet high school auditorium every year for about 15 years. Usually over a dozen schools from around the region joined

Tom, Vicki (Peschl), Meescha, and Andy Artzner (left to right).

us for the meat school. Sometimes I went to other towns in the area, like Brookings and Willow Lake, to hold meat schools. I even went to North Dakota once to put on a meat school for the high school agriculture teachers up there. I received quite a few awards and plaques from FFA for these meat schools.

Later on, I talked with high school classes about my time as a prisoner of war in Germany, but not at first. I told Marcie not to tell other people about my time as a POW because they might not understand what had happened to me. I always felt bad about being taken as a POW. I was afraid that some people might think I had just given up and wasn't brave enough to fight. Maybe some people did give up and jump the fence. During those days of fighting, I never shed a tear over what might happen to me because I knew that I was in the same boat as everyone else.

Howard Farr, Fred Peschl, Marcella Peschl, and Lois Farr (left to right).

Marcella Peschl, Joe Poplawski, Fred Peschl, and Ann Poplawski (left to right).

* * * * *

We built up the meat market to where we had more than 20 people working for us. Even John Morrell & Co. came up to see what I had because I was selling meat all over. But the State just got tougher than hell. If the state and federal hadn't changed regulations, maybe I'd still be in the meat business because I liked it. It wasn't that I didn't like it. I just didn't like the hassle. Three inspectors sat there all day telling me to do this and wipe that off.

They'd say to me, "Don't cook that one weinie on top. It's not done and these are too done." I knew that. They didn't have to tell me.

I'd say to them, "I'll just eat this one and let the other ones be." I'd get the other weinies out before they broke. I did things the old-fashioned way. I sold meat and it worked.

Armour's, Morrell's, and Flannery's wanted to see what I had here. I may have stepped into their territory, but I never knew we were doing that. I didn't think they'd care about a little place like this, but they did. I was getting up every day at 4:00 or 5:00 to go to work, and I was getting penalized for it.

I thought to myself, "What in the hell am I doing this for?" I tried to sell the business, but I couldn't get peanuts for it. I got so upset that I just thought, "Why don't I just quit?"

So the Friday before Memorial Day in 1973, I went over to the bank and said to Neil Meyer, "We've got 24 people working over there. I'm going to go back and I'm going to quit."

"You are?"

"Yup," I answered.

He asked, "What are you going to do if you quit?"

"I don't know." I said.

He was sympathetic with what I was feeling and said, "That's alright, Fred. I know you're having a bad time with all that inspection. Why don't you just quit? You'll think of something."

I said, "I'm going to go over and see Paul Green, the lawyer. I'll tell him to write a letter to the State." He wrote the letter and they got it special delivery. They got it the next Tuesday because Monday was Memorial Day. The inspectors came back Tuesday thinking I was going to do something, but we were locked up.

So I quit. I went back and I told Marcie then. I didn't even tell her before that. I told her I was quitting right now.

"I'm going to go back of the plant and you just watch the front. I'm going to take the girls back with me, too, and tell them all."

I went to the back room and said to the 24 workers, "We are going to quit today. Everyone here who wants to go on unemployment for 16 weeks can, because that's what you can get. Then you can look for a job. Some of you, I will definitely help to get a job. Some of you, I won't say anything bad; I just won't say anything. I'll just forget it. You just do what you can do." I didn't point anybody out, but they knew who I was not going to recommend to be a butcher or to work somewhere else.

Some of the workers like Ronnie Brown went out to the sign company in DeSmet. Combsie, Jim Comb's boy, he's out there, too. He was with me at that time. Richie Smith from the service station was another one. They were all good kids and good workers. They were kids who came after school and helped clean up. Another one was Skyberg who has the glass company over in Brookings. He was one of the younger ones. There was Earl Kickland. He did a good job on the saw or whatever he did. I recommended him highly for a job at Sunshine in Mitchell. I had Bernard Keiper. He was a minister in DeSmet, and he was really good. All the women who worked with us were great. All of my former employees still say, "Fred, we had the best time at your place that we ever had anywhere."

Bob Johnson was the first young man to come to work for us right out of high school. He turned out to be a very good butcher. He was left-handed and an excellent knife man. He went to Armour's in Huron to work. The foreman on the boning line told me that no one was faster or better than he was on their line.

But that's how I did it. I asked Rodney Zell and Lenora Holbert if they would stay with me until I get rid of all this stuff. I knew Rodney could deliver the meat that I still had left. Rod and Lenora always did a great job. I wasn't going to butcher any more. When you quit, you've got to stop butchering right away. All the meat that was in the building was inspected, so I didn't have to worry about that. And I didn't need the inspectors back anymore.

* * * * *

Then I started to sell meat equipment. The first big load I sold was of my own equipment. It included a brand new electronic scale that first came out 25 years ago. I sold it to a guy who was building a big grocery store in Superior, Wisconsin. He bought other things like the grinder and the big patty machine. I had just given $8,000 for that machine. He gave me the kind of money I wanted, and he knew he got a good deal too.

I decided to call some more locker owners. I called a couple from Nebraska. They said, "Well, what have you got, Fred." And I told them what I had.

"I'll get ahold of another man down here in Nebraska," he said, "I'll fly my plane and we'll come up and land in a field near DeSmet."

I said, "You can't land in the field. It isn't that good right now, but you can land in Huron. I'll have a guy there to pick you up." They came up and bought a semi load of butcher equipment too.

That's how I started to sell meat equipment. I was running out right away, so I just bought more. I just bought it and sold it. I bought equipment from one coast to the other. I sold it like anything. On some things I made mistakes, and on some things I did better. I didn't do everything right, but I didn't make it all wrong either. It worked out and after a while I just bought and bought and sold and sold.

Marcie said, "You're going to die with all of that equipment."

But I said, "I don't think so. I'll get rid of it all." Now I got rid of it all, and she can't believe it all sold.

* * * * *

Epilogue

I've had a lot of good luck all my life. I was lucky that Colonel Millett asked me to be his driver. That opened up many opportunities I wouldn't otherwise have had. I was lucky that a colonel invited me to see the Orange Bowl football game in Florida with him. It was just a coincidence that he would take me to the game and let me sit with him on the 50 yard line and buy me everything I wanted to eat. He even thanked me for being with him. I was lucky that the German officer in Frankfurt am Main sent me to Stalag Luft IV rather than to some other prisoner of war camp. I was lucky to get on the plane that went back to England with Howard Farr. The one I would have taken a few days earlier was shot down by the Germans. I was lucky that I didn't get killed on D-Day and that I survived being a POW. I was lucky to be able to get into the meat business in DeSmet. And I've been lucky to have a wonderful wife and children.

Looking back at these events, there's no doubt that I've been blessed. I've come to believe that my life has been more than luck. I'm supposed to do the right thing and make things good for others. That's what God wants me to do with my life. My faith has always been important to me. Joe Poplawski was Catholic. So were Art Schwegert, Howard Farr, and Bill Wixted. They helped me make it through the hard times.

People have been important to me all my life. Howard Farr and Art Schwegert were the main guys that I really knew from the service. A person can't go through any more than I did with Farr and Schwegert in that prison camp and on that march. We still went to see each other and visit together after it was all over. We were never at a loss for words. We never could just sit and not have something that we wanted to tell each other. It's just unbelievable.

One thing that I was very good at when I was in the equipment business was that I could talk. I'd talk about anything people wanted to talk about. If they wanted to talk about equipment, I could talk about equipment. If they wanted to talk about their dad in the service, I could talk about that, too. So I could talk either way. I hope that having this booklet and the things from the war in this shop will remind people of what others have done so they can have freedom.

Now that I'm retired, I'm just going to let people come in the store and look at what I've collected from World War II. I want to keep it kind of low key. I don't want to get it to where I have to work at it. I thought that if the kids from the high school want to come in and look at things, they'd find some things of interest. I want them to know that a person's family, their country, and their faith are the really important things in life. And that's what this book has been all about.

Chronology

May 24, 1919	Fred Peschl born in Yankton, South Dakota.
June 1938	Graduated from Yankton Public High School.
September 23, 1941	Married Marcie Schmidt.
May 6, 1942	Sworn into the U.S. Army.
August 1942	Arrived Ft. Benning, Georgia; made five jumps in Parachute School.
October 17, 1942	Graduated from Parachute School.
December 1942	Made 6th jump in Alabama.
December 1942	Went to Orange Bowl football game in Miami, Florida.
March 7, 1943	Arrived in Alliance, Nebraska; made 7th and 9th jumps.
July 3, 1943	Made 8th jump at the Denver Airport.
October 1943	Made 10th jump in South Dakota while on maneuvers.
November 1943	Arrived Camp Shanks, New York
December 2, 1943	Terry Peschl born in Yankton, South Dakota.
December 6, 1943	507th Airborn Infantry leaves New York harbor on the Stratenaver.
December 15, 1943	Landed in Liverpool, England.
December 22, 1943	Arrived in Belfast on the way to Port Rush, Ireland.
April 1944	Arrived at Tollerton Hall, England.

May 1944	Made 11th jump at Tollerton Hall, England.
June 4, 1944	D-Day postponed one day.
June 5, 1944	Paratroop planes took off for D-Day drops.
Tues., June 6, 1944	D-Day; made 12th and final jump.
Sat., June 10, 1944	Captured by the Germans.
August 4, 1944	Arrived by train at Stalag Luft IV near Gross Ttychow, Poland.
February 4, 1945	Prisoners at Stalag Luft IV began "the long march" across Germany.
March 29, 1945	Arrived at Fallingbostel, Stalag 357 and Stalag 11-B (about two mi. apart)
April 16, 1945	Liberated from Stalag 357 by General Montgomery's army.
April 23, 1945	Arrived at the hospital in Oxford, England.
June 6, 1945	Left England
June 22, 1945	Arrived in Newport News, Virginia, USA (Camp Patrick Henry)
May 8, 1945	WWII in Europe ends.
May 22, 1945	Arrived at Ft. Snelling, St. Paul, Minnesota and met Marcie and Terry.
May 24, 1945	Arrived with Marcie and Terry at home in Yankton, South Dakota.
September 1945	Went to Hot Springs, Arkansas for rest-and-recuperation.
September 29, 1945	Discharged from U.S. Army at Camp McCoy, Wisconsin.

January 9, 1946   Bought locker plant and meat market in DeSmet, South Dakota.
February 15, 1949 Vicki Peschl was born.
May 1973   Quit the meat market business and started the meat equipment business.

References Used and Other Recommended Materials

Brokaw, Tom. *The Greatest Generation*. 1998. New York: Random House, Inc.

Gorashko, Alexander. 1988. *Survival: The Ordeal of a Downed American Airman Held Captive in Germany's Stalag-Luft 4 and It's Infamous February Evacuation in World War II*. Also under the title *Kriegie*, Library of Congress Number TXU-217-013.

Ludden, Robert W. 1945. *Barbed Wire Interlude: A Souvenir of Kriegsgefangenenlager der Luftwaffe Nr. 4, Deutschland*. 116 South Pitt Street, Alexandria, VA.

Lyons, Michael J. 1994. *World War II: A Short History*, 2nd ed. Englewood Cliffs, NJ: Prentice Hall.

O'Donnell, Joseph P. 1982. *The Shoe Leather Express: The Evacuation of Kriegsgefangenen Lager Stalag Luft IV Deutschland Germany*. Ford Printing Company.

Peschl, Fred E. 1945. *A Wartime Log*. Personal collection, DeSmet, SD.

Rose, Leonard E. Hand-drawn depiction of Stalag Luft IV included in personal correspondence with Fred E. Peschl. Depiction also included in newsletter of the Indiana Chapter of American Ex-Prisoners of War, Inc., 8103 E. 60th Street, Indianapolis, IN 48226.

Sommers, Stan. 1980. *The European Story*. Packet No. 8 (July). American Ex-Prisoners of War, Inc. National Medical Research Committee, 1410 Alder Road, Marshfield, WI 54449.

Turbak, Gary. 1999. "Death March Across Germany." *VFW* (April): 30-34.

507th Parachute Infantry, 1943. Denver, CO: Bradford-Robinson Printing Co.

507th Parachute Infantry Regiment. *507th Regimental Combat History.* Reprinted 1983.

Experience WWII through the life of a D-Day paratrooper and POW

I'm "Fred": The Fred Peschl Story

Fred Peschl jumped as a paratrooper in Normandy on D-day and was captured a week later. Fred's book, **I'm "Fred"**, includes stories of training as a paratrooper, life as a prisoner of war, the "death march" across Germany, and liberation by the Allies. Fred describes his return to America to become a meat market owner and meat equipment businessman in a small South Dakota town.

I'm "Fred" is a must-have for a personal view of World War II. Great as a gift.

To order send check or money order to:
Fred Peschl Equipment Company
Box 33 — 213 Calumet Ave. SW
DeSmet, S.D. 57231

Yes! Please send *I'm "Fred"* to:

Name _____

Address _____

City _____ State ____ Zip ____

Number	Item	Cost
	I'm "Fred" ($7.00 each)	
	Postage and Handling ($2.00 per book)	
	Sales Tax (SD add 42¢ per book)	
	Total	

About the Author...

Fred Peschl was born and raised in Yankton, South Dakota, where he worked in a meat market. He was a paratrooper in the 507th Parachute Infantry on D-Day during World War II, and was captured by the Germans. He was placed in Stalag Luft IV, Poland, until February 1945 when the prisoners were forcibly marched during a bitterly cold winter and with very few provisions across Germany just ahead of the advancing Russian army. After the prisoners were liberated by General Montgomery, Fred returned to South Dakota to be reunited with his wife, Marcie, and year-old son. They purchased a meat market in DeSmet, South Dakota, which was later converted to a meat equipment business. Fred and Marcie currently live in DeSmet where they are active in church, school, and community.

ISBN 0-9673814-0-1